# How to Approach Death

Julia Tugendhat was a teacher before she trained to be a family therapist 20 years ago. In addition to writing 11 books for children under her maiden name of Dobson, she is the author of *What Children Can Tell Us About Divorce and Stepfamilies*, *The Adoption Triangle* and *Living with Loss and Grief*.

# Overcoming Common Problems Series

*Selected titles*

A full list of titles is available from Sheldon Press,
36 Causton Street, London SW1P 4ST, and on our website at
www.sheldonpress.co.uk

# Overcoming Common Problems Series

# Overcoming Common Problems Series

Overcoming Common Problems

# How to Approach Death

JULIA TUGENDHAT

First published in Great Britain in 2007

Sheldon Press
36 Causton Street
London SW1P 4ST

*British Library Cataloguing-in-Publication Data*
A catalogue record for this book is available from the British Library

ISBN-13: 978–0–85969–990–7
ISBN-10: 0–85969–990–0

1 3 5 7 9 10 8 6 4 2

Typeset by Northern Phototypesetting Co Ltd, Bolton
Printed in Great Britain by Ashford Colour Press, Hampshire

# Contents

*This book is dedicated to Sandra Jay*

# Introduction

The aim of this book is to provide practical information and advice on how to approach dying and death. We can all probably identify with Woody Allen, who is quoted as saying, 'I am not afraid of dying but don't want to be there when it happens.' A cursory perusal of books in a general bookshop graphically illustrates this head-in-the-sand attitude. The shelves are crammed with cheerful and informative books about pregnancy, birth and health. There are plenty of weighty academic studies on thanatology (the science of death) and many useful books on bereavement to help us deal with the deaths of others, but books on how to prepare for our own deaths are few and far between.

I hope this book will fill the gap. I will be focusing on the natural deaths of old people at the end of the life cycle. I shall not be covering the deaths of children or premature death in young and middle-aged adults. Such deaths, which are usually caused by accidents or terminal illnesses, fortunately make up a small proportion of overall deaths in the UK. Sadly, in other parts of the world where AIDS is rife this is not the case. Death and grief go hand in hand, as I will explain, but for a fuller understanding of bereavement I recommend readers to my previous book entitled *Living with Loss and Grief* (for details of all the books mentioned, see Further reading, p. **92**). I will discuss historical and current attitudes to death; the options we have for end-of-life care; the practical, psychological and spiritual ways we, and our carers, can try and make our own deaths as good as possible; and lastly, how to plan funerals and memorials.

Although I am 65 years old and a practising psychotherapist, as soon as I started my research I realized that I had not thought about my own death at all coherently, and certainly not out loud with close members of my family. I am probably rather typical. Having made a will some years ago, I stashed it away in a drawer and closed the subject of my old age, and in due course my inevitable death. Writing this book has enabled me to make a most interesting and enlightening personal journey. During the course of it, I have signed up as an organ donor, made a living will, recorded my funeral wishes, talked openly with my nearest and dearest, and reflected on my religious beliefs.

I just wish I had been able to read a similar book before my own parents died. Both their deaths were traumatic. I was not with them when they died and their funerals were miserable affairs. Their ashes were scattered in an unmarked section of a crematorium and they have no memorials. Now, when it is almost too late, I realize how much better it could all have been handled.

Fortunately I have also learnt that I can make one retrospective amend. I recently visited the crematorium where the hurried impersonal funerals of my parents had taken place. The manager was extremely kind and co-operative and was able to locate in a huge hand-written book the exact patch of ground where their ashes had been scattered. From the rough edge of this section I gathered a handful of earth – purely for its symbolic significance. I made contact with the vicar of the country church where my parents worshipped and he agreed to conduct a ceremony of remembrance for them. Their names and dates are now inscribed in a memorial book kept inside the church. I shall finally feel at peace when I am able to bring my grown-up children to see this book.

I have approached this subject from the perspective of an ordinary lay person and with the greatest humility. I am greatly indebted to everyone who has helped me make this journey and write this book. I could not have done it without the experts who have shared their knowledge with me, the professionals who have explained their work and the ordinary people who have given such honest descriptions of their experiences.

# 1

# Death

The way we have communicated about dying and death through time has reflected the sort of society in which we have lived. From medieval times to the nineteenth century, early death was such a commonplace occurrence that it was treated as part of the natural rhythm of life. Because death could strike down babies, children and adults alike at any time, the concept of mortality was very much alive. The duty of the Christian Church was to keep its flock in a state of readiness and awareness for the day when either the gates of Heaven would open for them or they would be consigned to the fire and brimstone of Hell. Images of the Grim Reaper as a skeleton carrying a scythe over one shoulder would have been familiar even to the masses who could not read. Illness and death were largely managed in the home so that bodily functions, diseases and corpses would have been familiar sights for everyone, including children. Pain and suffering not only had to be endured but were accepted as normal. It was understood that entering and leaving this life was a difficult undertaking. Our ancestors had no need of Ecclesiastes in the Old Testament to remind them that 'for everything its season, and for every activity under heaven its time: a time to be born and a time to die'.

The nineteenth century saw an explosion of medical, scientific, social and hygienic advances that greatly improved life expectancy. By 1901 this was 49 years for a woman and 45 for a man. Nevertheless, individuals were still intimately connected with the dying and regarded death as a familiar and natural event. Most people died in their own homes with their families around them. The corpse would be laid out in an open coffin in the front room where friends and neighbours would come and pay their respects. Fanny Trollope, the mother of the famous novelist Anthony Trollope, was typical of a woman in this era. Her husband, who was financially feckless, had bankrupted the family so often that Fanny had been forced to become the breadwinner by writing novels and travel books. During the space of two years she also nursed her husband and two children, who died of consumption. She snatched time to write in the early hours of the morning as she tended to them.

The big change in social attitude came about in the middle of the twentieth century, after two world wars, when dying and death ceased to be handled by the family and were transferred into the hands of professionals. The terminally ill were sent to hospitals to die. Medical advances were so exciting that the chief function of hospital doctors became the curing of disease and the saving of lives, with the result that dying patients were given minimal attention or special care. Visiting rights were so restrictive that people frequently died without their relatives around them. Their bodies were sent to undertakers, where morticians laid out and embalmed them. Funeral directors began to take over more and more of the funeral arrangements. Gradually, people became both physically and psychologically distanced from death, which was taking place out of our sight. Dying and death became something of a taboo subject.

Today, in our society, we have no problem about discussing dying and death in the public domain. In fact, it is now the subject of serious debate. In 2002, the life expectancy for a woman born in the UK was 81 years, compared to 76 for a man. By 2020 this is likely to be 84 and 79 respectively. By 2070, more than a million people in the UK will live to be over 100. New therapies, such as those using stem cells, may prolong life even more dramatically. The challenges and problems of an ageing population are being highlighted by the media. Think-tanks are grappling with the social and economic implications, and government is seriously worrying about the increasing demands for end-of-life care.

Our newspapers give us a daily diet of murders, accidents and suicides and we watch countless violent images of death on television and film. Yet when it comes to our own deaths, many of us are in a state of denial. The emphasis on health and longevity in our culture almost dictates that we are not supposed to die. Off the screen, most of us are unfamiliar with death. The advances of science and social changes have removed it from our daily experience. Few of us today will have witnessed an actual death or seen a corpse. There are some gullible people who believe that they can cheat death itself by having their bodies expensively stored in liquid nitrogen in the Cryonics Institute in the United States. Such people believe in the actual resurrection of the flesh through techniques of 'low temperature physics' that supposedly allow the preservation of corpses until some future day when they can be brought back to life.

Fortunately, the culture in which we seek to prolong life at all costs is now being seriously challenged. In common with a movement towards natural childbirth, there is a growing movement towards natural death. One of the first professionals publicly to articulate her concerns about the dying process was the Swiss doctor Elisabeth Kübler-Ross. When she went to work in the Manhattan State Hospital in 1958, she was so shocked by the way dying patients were treated that she spent the rest of her life trying to educate people about death. By forcing the American medical establishment to question the treatment of the dying, she did more than anyone else to push forward the hospice movement, palliative care and the notion of dying with dignity.

In Britain, the torch was taken up by Dame Cicely Saunders, who founded the hospice movement. She started her career as an almoner, then went into nursing and finally qualified as a doctor. She raised funds to build St Christopher's Hospice in Sydenham, which became the prototype for the hospice movement. The hospice took as its starting point the affirmation of death as a natural part of life, with the building designed to feel as informal and as homely as possible. The focus of medical attention was not cure but care combined with sophisticated pain relief. Resources such as family counselling and complementary therapies were provided to respond to the spiritual and psychological needs of the patients, which were considered as vital as the physical.

Since the foundation of St Christopher's in 1967, hospice care has grown into a worldwide movement that has radically changed the way we approach death and dying and is still having a significant influence on the provision and development of end-of-life care by the National Health Service (NHS). Palliative medicine has become recognized as an independent medical speciality, and palliative care is practised by nurses and doctors within hospices, hospice day centres, in people's own homes, in some hospitals, and by other professional groups in the NHS. Palliative care can be summed up as the active holistic care of patients with advanced progressive illness. It involves the management of pain and other symptoms and includes social and spiritual support to patients and their families.

The delivery of good palliative care in the community, in care homes and in hospitals has become an accepted political objective. The Gold Standards Framework (GSF) is being used as a model to improve supportive and palliative care in the community. The notion that we are all entitled to proper end-of-life care, which includes adequate support for family carers and the option of dying in the setting of our choice, has been recognized. There is now routine reference in public debate to the concepts of dying with dignity and the right to have a good death.

But what is a good death? Dying of old age tends to be a process rather than a sudden event. For death to occur, the failure of the brain, respiratory and circulatory systems must be irreversible. In his book *The Rights of the Dying*, David Kessler describes it in graphic terms as follows,

> Dying is like shutting down a large factory filled with engines and assembly lines and giant boilers. Everything does not suddenly go quiet when the 'off' switch is pushed. Instead, the machinery creaks and moans as it slows to a halt.

It is only natural for us to want to know what dying feels like, and it is only natural to want to believe that it will be a good rather than a horrible experience. As we cannot learn about death from the deceased themselves, we have to rely on descriptions given to us by those who have been close to death or witness to it.

Dr Kübler-Ross interviewed and observed the dying for many years. She learnt about feelings and fears from the terminally ill themselves and formulated her theories in her seminal book *On Death and Dying*. In the book she listed five stages through which, in her experience, the dying pass. The first is denial; the second, anger; the third, bargaining, in which the person tries to delay death; the fourth, depression, when the person realizes that the bargain is not working; and the last is acceptance. She described acceptance as the stage when the pain has gone, the struggle is over and the time has come for the final rest before the long journey. Death ought, she said, to be 'one of the greatest experiences ever'. She admitted that a few patients fight to the end and do not reach the acceptance stage, but by and large her experience taught her that old people die peacefully. 'It is a gradually increasing need to extend the hours of sleep very similar to that of the newborn child but in reverse order.' Although some experts have subsequently argued that the concept of five stages is too rigid, the research findings of Kübler-Ross have stood the test of time.

Books have been written with accounts of near-death experiences (NDEs) by people who have actually died for a very short time, or been at death's door before being revived. The Natural Death Centre, an educational charity which gives advice on death, dying and funeral provision, gathers research on NDEs in the belief that such experiences help people reconcile themselves to their own mortality. These NDEs seem to be remarkably similar. People describe being irresistibly drawn out of the body through a dark tunnel towards a bright welcoming light. Or they describe becoming disembodied, floating above but aware of the actions of those attending to them below. Sometimes they see loved ones waiting to welcome them.

For some people this is proof of life after death. Others provide physiological explanations for the phenomena: for example, the release of endorphins or oxygen starvation to the brain as the body shuts down. Whatever view is taken, it is comforting to know that nature has evolved a way of allowing dying humans to feel blissful. Someone I know, who had a cardiac arrest during a minor operation, claimed that nothing was easier than dying. Psychotherapist Carola Chataway described what happened to her in these words:

This experience, which I only later learnt to call a near-death experience, happened to me after I fell unconscious at home due to a clash of medications and was rushed into intensive care in hospital where my heart stopped beating for maybe two minutes. I wasn't expected to survive. When I did wake up many hours later, I had a very clear picture and memory of being pulled in a completely natural way from darkness behind towards an enormous all-embracing light and warmth. This didn't take place in a vacuum. I was being welcomed into another way of being that was unimaginable and amazing. Then I was very aware of a tug back – like a magnet pulling me away from this warmth and light which I wanted to reach but couldn't. When I woke up all wired to tubes, I remember asking the question (whether out loud or not I can't recall), 'What am I doing here? Why did you bring me back?' This experience affected me in two important ways. My life became very difficult afterwards but I had gained some sort of inner strength to cope with it. It was as if I had come back for a purpose, the reasons for which would become clear to me. And it has left me unafraid of death. Of course I would have regrets at leaving my children but the fear I had before is gone. I hesitate to say this for fear of incredulity but the feeling I had was of an all-encompassing radiance and quite simply the most glorious experience I have had.

What constitutes a good death seems to be a subjective judgement based on individual perspectives and beliefs, and may well be different for the person who dies and for the bereaved. Some people never know they are about to die because they are prematurely killed in an accident or trauma. The bereaved, who are feeling traumatized and shocked, might nevertheless regard this sudden death as good for the deceased because there was no suffering or long-term disability. Similarly, death from a massive heart attack, which is sudden and quick, may be good for the deceased but not for the survivors.

For religious believers, a good death is when the dying person has made peace with his or her soul, or undergone appropriate religious rites. The Catholic priest Father Mark Langham believes that there are three important elements of a good death that encompass the past, present and future.

> The first is when the dying person has a sense of a life fulfilled and has put his or her house in order and is at peace in this sense. The second is to be surrounded by love – with their loved ones there to help them on their journey. The third, is a sense of hope for the future with God, which is a precious thing for believers.

Muslims are taught that death is part of God's plan so they do their best to accept it philosophically. For Buddhists, Hindus and Sikhs, who believe in rebirth, this life is but a segment of a bigger plan. The next life will be affected by the way they live this one so it is important to strive for a tranquil death.

For some, death might only be accepted when every medical intervention has been tried and failed. For others, a good death might be a natural death, free of medical intervention. A dying person might prefer to make the final journey alone; another might want to be surrounded by friends and relatives. The way perspectives differ is well illustrated by the twentieth-century French philosopher Simone de Beauvoir in the book she wrote about her mother's death. She felt that her mother, who died in a nursing home of stomach cancer at the age of 78, had a dreadful death, despite the promise from the doctor that she would go out like a candle. De Beauvoir was even more bemused when a nurse assured her that it had been 'a very easy death', the title she ironically chose for her book. Her mother's death felt to her more like an 'unjustifiable violation' of nature.

It may be unrealistic to think that we can all have a good death. In his informative book *How We Die*, professor of medicine Sherwin Nuland cautions us not to have unreal expectations of a good death. He does not think there is much dignity or ease in the relentless disintegration of physical organs and feels that we would be better served by understanding this. A protracted and really painful death can happen and is terrible for the person who is dying and for the relatives. Even in our society some people still die in avoidable pain and distress. This has resulted in pressure building to allow the termination of the lives of patients who are dying in unbearable pain of a progressive illness. For such a termination, lethal drugs would need to be delivered directly by the doctor (euthanasia) or taken by the patient (assisted suicide). As euthanasia and assisted suicide are illegal in this country this would require a change in the law. Clearly, any move in this direction would have profound ethical and social implications.

Those who support assisted dying base their arguments on the principle of personal autonomy. They argue that a dying individual who is suffering has a right to die with dignity at a time of his or her choosing. They also argue that palliative care, while being an ex-cellent solution for many, is not always available. Those who are opposed to it use the first principle of the sanctity of life, which cannot in consequence be terminated by others, even on request. They also fear that it would be the beginning of the slippery slope to a wider use of euthanasia on vulnerable old people. They argue that improved palliative care with appropriate pain relief would make such a course unnecessary. With our ageing population and the capacity of technical intervention to prolong the process of dying, it is not surprising that euthanasia or assisted dying has become a hotly debated subject which will not go away, however much some people wish it would.

Current social surveys show that most of us in this country have reasonable expectations of what would constitute a good death. We want to be able to die free of pain, surrounded by family and in our own homes if possible. Being kept artificially alive without any quality of life is a real fear. 'I don't want to be lying in hospital like a vegetable, stuck with tubes, having been resuscitated,' is a common refrain. Some, if not all, of these objectives for a dignified death should be achievable today. At least we can try and inform ourselves of our end-of-life options and find out the best ways of getting our needs met, as well as doing what we can, as individuals, to prepare the way for a good death.

# 2

# Practical preparations for death

Natural death is usually preceded by a variable period of decline, infirmity and ill health. In 1814, one of the USA's Founding Fathers, Thomas Jefferson, vividly described the trials and tribulations of old age in a letter he wrote to another retired American president, John Adams:

> Our machines have now been running seventy or eighty years, and we must expect that, worn as they are, here a pivot, there a wheel, now a pinion, next a spring will be giving way, and however we may tinker them up for a while, all will at length surcease motion.

Today, in our society, old people can have their pivots, wheels and pinions changed and patched up by doctors who keep them going for considerably longer than in Jefferson's day. But inevitably, a time will come when physical and/or mental deterioration becomes obvious to ourselves and those around us. We begin to spend much more time in the doctor's surgery and hospitals. We may suffer from heart and arterial conditions like strokes, caused by narrowing and furring of the arteries, emphysema or respiratory diseases. For those over 65, circulatory disease is the most common cause of death. We may also get osteoporosis or arthritis in our bones, or cancer. Pneumonia as a cause of death also increases with age to account for one in ten deaths among those aged over 85. And because we are living longer, more of us are becoming senile before we die. This is a stage when some old people become frightened of dying and anxious about coping, especially if they have been in denial and have neglected to make advance plans or preparations. Rather than wait until we are on the threshold of death, we would be wiser to anticipate it while we are hale and hearty.

## Financial preparation

To start with, we should be making financial provision when we are young for our old age, which is likely to prove the most expensive phase of our entire lives. The high cost of end-of-life care can come as a shock. Old people tend to be very worried about money at this stage in their lives, and with good reason. Our pensions cannot cover the costs of a residential care home or private carers, so money has to be realized from capital sources, if they exist. Families who believe that end-of-life care will be funded by the state will be disappointed. Health care funded by the NHS is, of course, a free entitlement, but personal care, sometimes called social care, which is delivered by Social Services, is means-tested with variations between local authorities. If a Social Services assessment decides that what an old person is getting in a residential home is social rather than medical or nursing care, a financial contribution will be required. This often means selling a flat or house, which can cause a great deal of distress to the old person who worked hard to buy it, as well as to the family who hoped to inherit it.

The border line between social care and health care is a blurred and contentious one that has given rise to several legal cases. Making us contribute to our own end-of-life care after we have paid taxes for years might seem unfair, but it may be unrealistic to expect the state fully to fund a rapidly growing aged population. We would be well advised to seek early financial advice about life insurance schemes, insurance to cover loans, ways of mitigating inheritance tax and raising income against our property. We should also avoid making such generous provision for children, in order to save inheritance tax or for other reasons, that we leave ourselves short at the end of our lives. Help the Aged runs a Care Fees Advice Service offering free financial advice on how to meet the costs of on-going care.

## Making a legal will

I strongly recommend making a will for anyone who is married or is in a civil partnership, who has children or who has no close relatives. I would go even further and say that it is a moral duty to do so. Some 600,000 people die in the UK every year. Of these, only one in four makes out a legal will. This is astonishing, considering the number of problems that may occur when someone dies intestate. Most people know about wills and intend to make one, but never get around to it. They may believe that they have too few possessions or money to make a will worthwhile. Or they may not bother because they think their possessions will go to the family anyway. Even though making a will need not be complicated, as I hope to illustrate, some people are put off by the administrative and legal aspects. But the fundamental problem may well be a psychological one. Avoidance is a form of denial. By signing a will, we are formally acknowledging that one day we are going to die.

On one level, making a will can be rather a dry legalistic exercise. On other levels it can be a creative and informative exercise, full of meanings and opportunities. Making a will can provide an opportunity for us to sit down and discuss the terms and implications of our wishes; to clarify our feelings for our nearest and dearest; and to prompt new thoughts and plans for the future. We are given the opportunity, in a formal way, to show love and gratitude or to make amends. We can express our trust in friends by appointing specific individuals as executors who will be responsible for carrying out (executing) the directions expressed in the will. Instructions for our funerals and memorials can also be included in our wills. Marguerite told me how she and her husband discovered what values they shared when they made their wills.

> When my husband and I drew up our wills some years ago, we agreed on two important principles. We decided that it was more important for us to save and spend our money on leading independent lives to the end if possible, rather than striving to leave money to the children. In other words, we do not want to be a burden on them. The other principle is that of equal division of possessions. We happen to have one high-earning son, and a daughter who earns very little. When we have helped them financially with this and that we have always done the same for both. We have a bad example in our family of an unfair will which has split siblings apart and which will have reverberations for generations to come. We did not want to make the same mistake.

We can make a will by doing it ourselves or by using the services of a bank or solicitor. Home-made wills are not recommended, but should this path be taken, the best course is to use standard forms which can be purchased from stationers like W. H. Smith, or *Which?* The form must be signed in the presence of two individuals who are not beneficiaries or married to beneficiaries. Most of the major high street banks can provide advice on wills and the administration of estates. A bank may be competent to give advice on inheritance tax and can act as executor as well as dealing with probate, which is the legal right to administer the estate.

Wills are commonly drawn up by solicitors. A solicitor can also act as executor, administer the estate and hold the original will. It is well worth enquiring about charges. Banks tend to charge more than solicitors. Among solicitors, charges can vary enormously according to the complexity of the will and the standing of the firm.

At least one executor needs to be appointed to administer a will. An executor can be a beneficiary under the estate, a member of the family, a trusted friend or a professional such as a solicitor or bank manager. The role of the executors is to ensure that the terms of the will are carried out properly. Usually this task is straightforward and undemanding, but I have known of several cases of disputed wills where the executors have found themselves caught up in a complicated and time-consuming legal process.

Wills describe how our assets should be distributed after we are dead. We can leave legacies to charities or anyone we like, as well as personal items, such as jewellery and pictures, to named individuals.

At the same time as making a will, it might be sensible to give Enduring Power of Attorney (EPA) to someone we trust. This authorizes them to take business and other decisions on our behalf if we cease to be mentally competent. Although this power is unlikely to be exercised until the very end of life, the time to arrange it is when we are still in full possession of our mental faculties. Giving an EPA does not prevent a person managing their own affairs while capable.

The Citizens Advice Bureau (CAB) and the Law Society can provide names of reputable local solicitors. The Royal National Institute for the Blind (RNIB) has a guide on making and changing wills in Braille.

Should someone die intestate (without making a will), the legal complications can be lengthy and complicated. Without a nominated executor matters will take longer to settle, which might leave a survivor in sore need of cash. The individual's assets will be distributed according to a rigid legal formula which may jeopardize a partner's security and may not be what was really intended. Intestacy may also lead to unnecessary or excessive payments of inheritance tax. An unmarried partner might even have to take legal action to obtain a share of the assets. Further repercussions may affect charitable bequests. If a gift to a charity is made in a will it is exempt from inheritance tax, but without a will all assets are liable to be taxed unless they pass to a tax-exempt beneficiary under the general law (for example, a widow), with the result that the main beneficiary is HM Revenue and Customs.

Having drawn up a will, we find it only too easy to stick the envelope in the back of a drawer and forget about it. Solicitors generally recommend that wills be updated every five years. Our assets may have diminished, beneficiaries may have died or fallen out of favour, and our own needs or priorities may be different. Tricia's tale is a cautionary one.

After my first marriage broke down and I lived on my own for some years, I met a wonderful man who was also divorced. We had ten blissful years together before he contracted inoperable cancer. It was very difficult watching him die so painfully, but by the end of his long and courageous struggle with illness I was ready to let him go. Although he had told me that he had left me well provided for, when we unearthed his will I discovered that he had left his entire pension to his first wife. Not only had she made him very unhappy but she was significantly wealthier than I am. The whole business was extremely distressing because I was left with so many unanswered questions. Had he just forgotten to update his will? If he loved me so much how could he have made such an oversight? Did he still have feelings for his ex? Was he so guilty that he felt a need to compensate her? I was left feeling really angry.

## A living will

A Living Will or Advance Healthcare Directive is another document worth considering well in advance. It contains our wishes regarding future medical treatment and intervention when we have become incapable of communicating these wishes ourselves. The main purpose for making an Advance Directive is to stop our lives being artificially sustained or prolonged by treatment which has become futile and burdensome. Formal Advance Directives can be obtained for a small cost from Age Concern, Dignity in Dying and the Natural Death Centre. We can also write out our own wishes and get these signed and witnessed. Advance Directives are legally binding, but only as long as they are specific to the given clinical situation. General statements like 'I do not wish to be artificially kept alive' are not binding, and therefore it is safer to use a printed form which requires answers to specific questions about resuscitation and tube-feeding. We may appoint a trusted relative as a Healthcare Proxy so that he or she can communicate our wishes on our behalf. And the government is proposing a Lasting Power of Attorney (LPA) which will permit an individual to appoint a trusted person to protect his or her interests in decisions about personal care. This builds on current law that allows an appointed person to take care of a mentally incompetent individual's financial affairs.

However, an Advance Directive is no substitute for verbal communication. As long as we are conscious and know what is going on, we have the right to be given information about our medical condition, and we have the right to refuse further treatment. We can verbally communicate our end-of-life wishes to a doctor or a nurse who should record them in the patient notes. We can also discount any advance wishes we have made on paper and request to be resuscitated or tube-fed. Our hold on life is very strong and what we thought we wanted years earlier may not fit any longer.

Sometimes relatives do not know what to do for the best when their loved one is unconscious. They may want treatment to be prolonged because they are not ready to let go. An Advance Directive could be helpful in this situation. The Healthcare Proxy can communicate our wishes at the crucial moment of decision. We should give a copy of the Advance Directive to our GP, our next of kin and to the Proxy if we appoint one.

## Organ donation

Another key question we need to ask ourselves, however morbid it may seem, is whether we want to be an organ donor when we die. The need for organs far outweighs their availability, and every year hundreds of people die while waiting for a transplant. Most transplants are successful, and because of the ageing population the number of people needing one, especially a kidney, is rising. At the same time, a drop in the number of road accidents and advances in medical treatment have led to a decline in the number of donated organs. Although many old people believe that their organs will be too worn out to be useful, it should be noted that there is no age limit to organ donation, though organs will obviously not be used if they are unsuitable. It is possible to transplant healthy kidneys, livers, corneas, tissue and bone from old people who die. The oldest patient to donate a kidney was 86, and corneas were transplanted from a donor who was 101 years old.

There are lots of reasons why we are reluctant to sign up as donors, even though we may agree with the general principle. We may feel squeamish about our bodies being dissected after death. Some people fear that if they are identified as donors, doctors and nurses will not strive to keep them alive, or that their body parts will be removed before they are dead. All these fears are unjustified. Organs are only removed for transplantation after a person has been certified brainstem dead by two doctors entirely independent of the transplant team, who are then obliged to carry out the procedures speedily and with dignity. Some people, for example strict Jews and Muslims, will not consider organ donation because of their religious principles.

A common reason for the shortage of donors in the UK is that we don't get down to organizing it. Carrying around a donor card is not really sufficient. Cards get mislaid or may not be to hand when death occurs. The most effective way to become a donor is to sign up to the NHS Organ Donor Register, either via the internet or by writing to UK Transplant. Those who want to donate their whole bodies for medical research should obtain information from the Human Tissue Authority, who will direct them to an appropriate medical school in their area for further details. There is a shortage of bodies for research and inquiries are welcomed. There is no age limit but there are criteria for acceptance and all details need to be understood and organized beforehand. The UK Parkinson's Disease Society Brain Tissue Bank welcomes donated brain tissue from those with the disease, and also normal brain tissue for control purposes. All arrangements, however, must be made before death.

Confidentiality throughout the donation process is always maintained, though the families may want to exchange anonymous letters of thanks or good wishes through transplant co-ordinators. I have read many stories on the internet of donor and recipient families who have met and become friends. Relatives of donors can draw great comfort from the knowledge that the death of a loved one has brought life and joy to others. A mother of a young man who was killed in a car accident expressed her feelings like this:

> My son's death was so utterly senseless. One minute he was full of life; the next he was dead. I like to think of some of his energy and positive spirit continuing in the lives of others, strangers though they are.

Generally, recipients are so grateful for a new lease of life that they try to live as healthily and responsibly as possible. It was disappointing to learn that the recently deceased footballer George Best had gone on drinking after receiving a liver transplant.

A kidney transplant liaison nurse at a leading London hospital has strong views about donation:

> I think it is selfish not to register to be an organ donor. We have enough organs in our bodies to save or improve the lives of 10 to 15 people after we are dead. I work in the health service and feel it is my moral duty to be on the register.

I do not believe that anyone should be morally coerced into donating bits of their bodies or those of their loved ones. The thought of helping someone in need can give comfort to the bereaved, but it can also feel morally wrong. However, by giving the matter serious consideration we will become clear, either way, whether we want to donate or not.

Having made our decision, it is vital that we share it with those who will be most involved in our demise. Some awkward and damaging scenes have arisen at death beds when family members have had differing views over the dead person's wishes on this sensitive subject. Until quite recently, even in the case of registered donors, organs could not be removed without the consent and co-operation of relatives. The Human Tissue Act of 2004 now makes the wishes of the donor paramount by making it lawful to remove organs or tissue even if this does not accord with the wishes of relatives. Nevertheless, relatives will be far better psychologically if they are fully aware of the wishes of the deceased.

There is no doubt about the benefits to relatives of unambiguous and clearly written instructions and wishes. Everyone knows stories of post-death disputes and rifts. I certainly have some unedifying examples in my own extended family. Advance preparation cannot always prevent these from happening, but unequivocal clarity can often save a lot of heartache among relatives. In later chapters, I will show how wills, organ donation and funeral wishes are actually carried out after death.

By making advance preparations for our deaths, we not only benefit our relatives in the future, but we benefit ourselves in the present. Death is an unknown and frightening concept and we have no way of knowing how we will respond to it. And what lies beyond it can only be imagined. Some old people are sustained by their belief in an afterlife, but few appear to embrace death with the fervour of John Donne, the great seventeenth-century poet and preacher, whose commissioned portrait showed him wrapped in a funeral shroud. I suspect that, if we allow ourselves to think about the matter at all, most of us are anxious and frightened about dying and death. In Father Mark's experience a particular fear is that of dying alone.

Yet as we grow old we cannot avoid being aware of death on a conscious and unconscious level. We may have taken the deaths of our parents in our stride but the death of friends and contemporaries comes as a huge shock. We can go on as if nothing is happening or we can start making conscious preparations for the inevitable. My experience as a psychotherapist has taught me that fears and anxieties are invariably reduced when articulated and addressed. Therefore, I am confident that by making advance psychological and practical preparations we can reduce and contain our nebulous fears about dying and death.

# 3

# Arranging a funeral in advance

Planning our own funerals can be an enlightening exercise for ourselves and will be extremely helpful for our relatives who have to make the arrangements when we die. A funeral is an important occasion for family and friends to support one another and a crucial part of the grieving process. The more it reflects the life and beliefs of the deceased, the more it will be harmonious, coherent and a comfort to the bereaved.

By this stage in my life I have become quite a connoisseur of funerals, and I have to say that some have been lovely and others rather horrible. I have experienced services in crematoria which have been hurried and impersonal. The music has been canned, the pall bearers have looked like tailors' dummies, the service has been taken by a minister who obviously did not know the deceased, and the mourners have scurried off as if they could not get away fast enough. I have also been to the most uplifting funerals where the local choir has sung comforting hymns, where grandchildren have read their own poems, and where the minister has given an intimate address.

The choice of our own funeral is worth considering in advance because there are now so many more options than formerly. Ken West, who has been involved in bereavement services for over forty years, described some of the changes he has seen during his working life.

Funerals used to be traditional stolid affairs, based on Christian principles. Ministers tended to be very orthodox and unsympathetic to unconventional ideas. Today people are considering more personalized alternatives. Many of these are along more environmentally friendly lines. Bereavement services are learning to be much more sensitive to cultural and individual needs.

## Cremation

Cremations comprise 70 per cent of all funerals in the UK. There are some 240 crematoria, mostly owned by municipal authorities although a few are in private hands. Burials used to be the norm until the nineteenth century, when cremations grew in popularity, at first among the wealthy and professional classes. Cremation was seen as an insurance against being buried alive. In previous centuries there had been enough stories of this happening to leave a real horror of the possibility. Occasionally, bells were attached to coffins, just in case such a fate befell someone who then needed to raise an alarm. Burials were viewed as old-fashioned, cremations as modern and hygienic. Many cemeteries had become derelict and overgrown and cremation was seen as an economical use of space. In fact, the motto of the Cremation Society, which promoted cremations, was 'Save the land for the living'. Crematoria were custombuilt, with chapels, waiting-rooms and landscaped gardens.

Nowadays, there are several advantages to a cremation. It is cheaper than burial, which can be a significant consideration. Some people find the idea of being burnt to ashes more appealing than rotting in the earth. Ashes are easily transportable and can be buried or scattered wherever we choose – on the top of mountains, in rivers or in meadows. They can also be put in caskets and buried formally in a churchyard, or informally in a garden or orchard. The portability of ashes is an advantage in our mobile society, when our work may take us miles from our birthplace.

The disadvantages of cremation are the soulless and standardized features that made it so popular with the Victorians. While it was once regarded as a modern and sanitized process, today we worry about the carbon dioxide and mercury emissions caused by the firing process. A fast-freezing technique is presently being developed where a body is frozen and then shattered into biodegradable ash. If the technique became efficient and economical it would provide a solution to cremation emissions.

## Burial

Christianity is still the dominant religion in the UK. Anyone whose permanent address is within the parish, whether Christian or not, is in theory entitled to be buried in the parish churchyard, even if the death took place elsewhere. In practice, however, there may well be no room as many church cemeteries in the countryside are full or disused. Some now will only accept ashes, which take less room. Even the larger municipal cemeteries are finding it harder to accommodate bodies. The shortage of space is so serious that the government is contemplating double burials. Under the proposal, untended graves older than 75 years would be reopened. The remains would be transferred to a smaller container and reburied deeper in the same plot, leaving room for a new coffin on top.

For some people, one of the advantages of being buried is that it feels more natural to allow a body to rot in the earth.

Churchyards can be tranquil, beautiful and havens of wildlife. Because so many of them are old, they are redolent with history.

A significant advantage of a grave with a headstone is that it provides a fixed location for the bereaved. The daughter of a friend has begged her not to be cremated because she wants to be able to visit her mother's grave with her children and, eventually, grandchildren. There is also much more scope for individual headstones than in a crematorium.

Richard Dorment recently purchased a double burial plot for himself and his wife in his local cemetery, Kensal Green in London. He first thought about arranging his own funeral after a friend told him what a tremendous help it had been to her after her husband died to find that he had planned everything down to the last detail.

This got me thinking about my own two children who live abroad. They are unfamiliar with the infrastructure of this country and would not know what to do if we died. We thought it would really help them if we did all the arrangements in advance. We chose burial rather than cremation because we both find cremation services very lowering. A burial seems more real and natural somehow. We chose Kensal Green because it would be convenient for the children to visit if they wanted to put flowers on the grave. We walked round the Victorian section until we found a spot we liked. We were careful to avoid overhanging trees because bird shit ruins a grave in no time. The plot cost £1,200 in perpetuity, which does not seem unreasonable.

Then we turned our attention to the tombstone. As an art critic and historian, aesthetics mean a great deal to me. We did not want any old headstone made up so we consulted a well-known stone engraver and had him make a design for us. Choosing what words we wanted inscribed on the stone proved fascinating. It required us to sum up who we were in very few words. We have even specified it be made from Cumbrian grey stone. Some materials like white marble get horribly dirty and eroded. The design has been drawn on a full-scale cartoon which is rolled up in a cardboard cylinder. This is kept in a drawer in my desk with my will and my funeral wishes. I do not want a memorial service. I want a simple funeral mass and burial and then I want everyone to come back to the house for champagne and good food. In this folder I have also left letters to the children and a few special things like childhood recipes. I used to make them Great Aunt Lily's spaghetti sauce and I like the idea of them making spaghetti dinners when I am gone.

Burials at sea are possible for those who like the idea of being consigned to the deep. An application for the necessary licence should be made to the Department for Environment, Food and Rural Affairs (DEFRA) or to DEFRA's local District Inspector of Fisheries. The application must include the death certificate and a certificate from a doctor to state that the body is free of infection. The body cannot be embalmed (embalming is the process usually performed by undertakers which involves replacing the blood in the arterial system of a dead body with a preservative, normally a solution of formalin; it delays decomposition but has no long-term preservative value). It should be clothed in biodegradable garments, and two plastic identity tags must be attached to it. The coffin needs to be constructed to certain specifications and must be weighted. In England there are presently three burial sites: one off the Isle of Wight, one near Tynemouth and the other near Newhaven on the south coast. Any boat can be used provided it has navigational instruments.

The disadvantage of a burial at sea is that there is a risk of the coffin, or the body, being washed back to the shore or caught up by trawlers. The Marine Fisheries Agency will give advice and information if asked, and the Britannia Shipping Company for Burial at Sea Ltd is a specialist undertaker.

Scattering ashes at sea is a less complicated option. No licence is needed, so people can go out in small boats and scatter the remains wherever they want.

## Green burial

We are more ecologically aware than we used to be. This is one reason why woodland or natural burials are increasing in popularity. They appeal to people who want to be buried in beautiful rural settings, with minimum fuss and without adding to the pollution of the atmosphere. There are now about 200 such sites in the UK. A natural burial site consists of a leased acreage of woodland, pasture or parkland which is specially designated for burials.

Those who choose a green burial must abide by a few eco-friendly rules. The body should not be embalmed. Only simple shrouds or biodegradable coffins made of cardboard, bamboo or willow can be used, so that everything can decompose naturally. No marble or stone headstones are allowed, although on some sites trees can be planted or simple wooden crosses erected. The whole point is for the site to be as natural as possible.

It is becoming a vogue in Australia to be buried in a vineyard. This must give pleasure to the family of someone who has enjoyed good wine.

A natural funeral can be organized by the family, but it can also be partially or fully organized by a funeral director and can be conducted with full religious rites. Cathy had such a good experience of her first natural burial that she wants one for herself when the time comes.

> I went with a friend about a year before she died to look at the South Downs Natural Burial Site. She liked the site and so this is where we all turned up when she died. It was a lovely late August day with the sun shining through the woods. About eighty of us gathered in a building at the top and joined in a service taken by a vicar who had been her friend. There was live music and chanting. One person talked about her and another read out an Indian poem about friendship. She had been laid in a willow coffin which appeared blue because it had been entwined with sweet-smelling lavender. This was put on an old-fashioned wooden bier on wheels which was bumped down through the woods to the sound of music and chanting. We all threw lavender sprigs on top of the coffin, which was lowered into the ground. She would have loved the ceremony – it was so individual, so 'her'. Now there is a silver birch to mark the spot.

A few people have cited unfortunate experiences with natural burials. Descriptions of sites have been misleading, and the administration lamentable. I read of a family who turned up on the day to find the grave had not been dug. It is therefore very important to visit and choose a natural burial site early on. Check that the operator of the site is a member of the Association of Natural Burial Grounds, whose members adhere to a strict code of conduct.

The law requires the management of a burial site to keep a register of every interment and a plan to indicate where the bodies have been buried. Some relatives are happy for the body of their loved one to merge with others on the same site, but others want to be able to relocate the exact site in the future, especially if they intend to plant a memorial tree. It is therefore important to have access to a ground plan. A few burial grounds will provide a microchip which is interred with the body and can be activated by a relative who wants to locate the exact position of a loved one.

## A family-arranged funeral

A DIY or family-arranged funeral that does not involve a funeral director is another option. This should not be confused with a green burial, although the two are often combined. A DIY arrangement assumes that the family will purchase a coffin, collect the body with their own bearers and deliver it in their own transport to the church or crematorium at a prearranged time. They will contact a minister and arrange all the details of the service. Until quite recently, such a request would have been unsympathetically treated as crackpot. Today, however, most funeral directors, crematoria and pastors will advise and co-operate with families who want to be much more closely involved in the arrangements themselves. The undertaker could be contracted to provide some of the services – for example, the use of their mortuary and a hearse – while the family does all the rest.

A funeral organized and carried out by the family can be significantly more economical. Another advantage is that the bereaved derive solace and satisfaction from being in control. But a DIY funeral is a challenging event to organize: many things can go wrong, and someone has to be strong enough to be in charge of the numerous details. Guidance and advice can be obtained from the Natural Death Centre, which is supportive of cheap family-arranged funerals. It has produced an excellent and practical manual, *The Natural Death Handbook*, which offers advice on green burials, including available sites. It provides a list of recommended funeral directors, crematoria and cemeteries.

The burial of Princess Diana in the grounds at Althorp, her childhood home, made the idea of home burials rather fashionable. Why not be buried in the back garden? It sounds like an attractive idea but is probably not advisable except on a big country estate. Permission from the local planning office and environmental health department must be sought, and other practical considerations need to be taken into account. A body in the garden will bring down the value of the house. If the family moves, as it well might, the body cannot be exhumed without special permission. Strictly speaking, a buried casket of ashes is also subject to exhumation laws but in reality can be more easily moved without permission.

Funeral and burial costs vary considerably according to region. Cremations are usually cheaper than burials. Those who are worried about the cost falling on their families or who have specific funeral wishes might consider paying in advance. A pre-paid funeral plan can be drawn up with an undertaker, or a sum of money for the funeral invested in a Building or Friendly Society. Another option is to take out a life insurance policy specifically related to funeral expenses. Ken West's general advice about arranging a funeral is straightforward:

> Don't leave all the decisions about your funeral for your relatives to take after you are dead. And do try and talk to your children about these decisions. This would give great comfort to many elderly people. Many problems and upsets occur when relatives disagree over funeral arrangements or what to do with the ashes. Even if the deceased made his wishes known, the relatives are not obliged to execute them. For instance, relatives might find the use of a cardboard coffin unseemly, or organ donation abhorrent. Leaving specific instructions might not prevent family rows, but at least there will be no argument about the interpretation of intentions.

## Advance Funeral Directive

Funeral wishes can be added to the will, written out informally or incorporated in a document called an Advance Funeral Directive which can be obtained from Age Concern, Dignity in Dying, *Which?* or local cemeteries and crematorium services. This form is not legally binding but provides a structure for detailed planning of a funeral. It covers issues such as whether we wish our bodies to be kept at home until the funeral, and whether we want to be embalmed and our bodies viewed after death. We can be specific about whether we want flowers or charitable donations. For some people the most important thing is to state their religious or non-religious beliefs and how they want the funeral service conducted. Completing an Advance Funeral Directive is a most instructive exercise because it makes us think about our values and beliefs.

After obtaining and filling out these forms we will probably have learnt a great deal about ourselves and will also have had some helpful conversations with our relatives at the same time. Finally, we can do them a real favour by putting our wills, funeral directives and all the details like insurance numbers and birth certificates that will be needed after we die in one clearly labelled file which is kept in an accessible place.

A final preparatory task which may have more appeal is that of passing on our history and life stories while we can, as a way of preserving our identity and claiming a place, however minor, in history. In the year before they died, Jefferson and Adams commiserated with each other about having their death masks taken. The process, to which they both submitted with surprisingly good grace, was very unpleasant. Layers of grout were plastered over their faces and left to dry before being removed by chisel and hammer. These masks tell us what they looked like as old men, and their volumes of letters tell us a great deal about their personalities. Today, alas, letter writing is a dying art. I consider this a great loss because letters have proved such valuable historical documents.

Fortunately, we have other media at our disposal. We have photography, film and audiotape. The only record I have of my grandparents is a series of formal studio photographs, but today grandparents and great aunts can be seen in action on the family camcorder. Even old photos can be turned by technicians into DVDs. I was invited to a splendid eightieth birthday party for a woman who had led a fascinating youth in Kenya. We were shown a video incorporating old grainy photos interspersed with live commentaries from contemporaries and relatives. This is not only good archive material but a precious memorial for her family. The young may not show much interest in our lives immediately, but they may well in time. Family genealogy has become a popular pursuit on the internet. Each generation tends to throw up one guardian of the family history. Our memories, whether written down, or recorded, will be greatly appreciated, and in the act of reminiscing we too will gain a new understanding and insight into our lives. Claus Moser, who has been awarded a peerage for distinguished public service, told me what the process of reminiscing on audiotape at the age of 83 has meant to him.

I decided to make an audio recording because increasingly my three children and nine grandchildren kept on asking me about my past – especially in relation to Hitler and Nazi Germany. They wanted to know what it was like coming to Britain as a refugee at the age of 13. I realized that my life has been interesting and I thought it would be a good process for understanding myself better. I do not feel entirely English, or German. I feel vaguely European. I am Jewish but not practising.

Having decided to do it, I then had to work out how it should be done. One option was to write it down, which I did not want to do. Another option was to allow myself to be interviewed by an outsider. The option I chose was to do a joint interview with my older brother, with whom I am very close, with my academic daughter and my brother's son as the interviewers. We realized that they would be good interviewers because they really wanted to know, because it is their background too. And it made for a degree of depth and honesty that we had never expected. We agreed on two rules only. Nothing was off limits. And we would start with our births and end in 1946.

We started by questioning each other and triggering our mutual memories. Very quickly the interviewers started interrupting with questions. We did nine hours of recording which we will edit and put in a nice booklet for each member of the family.

What came out of it? First were the facts. I would have forgotten so much but my brother has a better memory and together we filled in the facts of our lives in Berlin and when we came to England. We filled out the family tree with the relatives my children had never met who had been sent to concentration camps. As we got more relaxed, we learnt so much about the emotions we had probably suppressed – how we felt about what had happened to us. Through this extraordinary process we learnt so much about each other.

Some friends have subsequently suggested that it was an arrogant and self-centred thing to do. I do not agree with them. We are very happy with the result. I feel that I am bequeathing something that will help our children to understand our lives. The prize for me was when my daughter said, 'I now understand you much better.'

# 4

# Death talk

While the elderly are making preparation for their deaths they may talk to friends of the same age and to professionals, but death talk is very often a taboo subject in the bosom of the family. The young are adept at avoiding painful subjects. When an old person tries to talk about death, a typical response might be, 'Oh, please don't talk about such a gloomy subject. You aren't going to die for ages.' In addition they don't want to be misinterpreted or thought to be in a hurry to inherit. They find it distressing to think about life without a beloved relative and at some level fear that speaking of it might bring it nearer.

From their perspective, parents want to protect their children from their own anxieties and fears. They in their turn do not want to cause distress and may already be feeling that they are too much of a burden. Most of the very old people I spoke to gave me a similar story: 'I can't talk to my children about my death. They won't hear of it.'

It may be easier for the older generation to initiate death talk. If children and grandchildren hear us talking about death in a natural way, they have permission to do the same. A good place to start is early on, when we are making our wills and it feels natural to discuss the practical arrangements we are making. The longer the discussion is avoided, the more difficult it becomes. Cathy, who enjoyed her friend's natural burial, talks about death with her children as naturally as she talks about any other subject.

> Whenever we go on a holiday, I ring up my grown-up son and daughter to tell them how much I love and value them, just in case something happens and we don't come back. We have given them our living wills and they know what our funeral wishes are. My son says he wouldn't mind having my skull on his desk like they used to do in the old days.

In much the same vein, I have friends who remind each other of potential death when they feel quarrelsome by saying 'Last day' to each other. By keeping alive the notion that this might be our last day we can avoid saying things that we would so regret if death occurred after a quarrel.

Many a religious prayer contains a reminder of death. Catholics, for instance, are reminded of their own mortality when they recite the Hail Mary, which ends with the words, 'now and at the hour of our death'.

For others, though, the subject of death can be off limits right to the very end. The taboo might continue even if someone is manifestly dying. Deidre is certain that denial was the right course for her husband, who spent the last five years of his life being cared for at home, though she never denied the knowledge to herself. The GP who visited knew his patient well and talked about symptoms without mentioning the word 'death'.

> Malcolm was extremely unwell, especially in the last two years, with various heart and circulation problems and a viral condition which attacks the muscles. The key to my approach was we never discussed the fact that he was dying because he never wanted to. He had always said to me, 'If I am dying I don't want to know. I am not one that needs to be told I have six months to live.' We were always talking about his next project and activities. He had a tremendous life force and optimism which kept him going.

The writer and broadcaster Daisy McAndrew gave a very different account of her father's death in January 2006. Alistair Sampson spent the last two weeks of his life in a hospice where he entertained a stream of visitors, including his dog, in his room. Those he could not see he telephoned to say goodbye. He planned his own funeral service, choosing a collection of his favourite tunes from musicals and funny poems he had written himself. According to a newspaper article written by Daisy shortly after his death,

> Hospice staff answered our endless questions with patience and no-nonsense good humour. They never patronized my father or anyone else in the family and managed to make the process dignified and special – without ever trying to 'cheer us up'.

There is less possibility for denial in a hospice because the reason people are there is so clearly understood. They are there because they are terminally ill and they know that the task of the hospice is to ease them through the dying process. Support and advice are also given to relatives during the illness and afterwards. This can be particularly useful if the bereaved are young children. Sometimes it needs a small amount of sensitive facilitation by a professional to free everyone to talk about the subject that is on everyone's mind.

Sometimes, a dying person will feel too protective to talk to a partner but will be able to talk to someone else in the family, a friend or a pastor. I was moved by the description 30-year-old Ann gave me of the last conversations she had with her dying grandmother, who spent the last year of her life in a nursing home.

> We were able to talk very openly about everything. I think she was somehow cleaning up her memories so that she could leave this life. I was able to tell her that I felt she had ignored me as a child. I didn't think we had got on until I was in my teens. She then told me about all the memories she had of me as a baby and I was comforted. We understood each other so well during these last months. I knew she trusted my decisions and my way of doing things. Her last words were, 'I think I've made it.' And that's what I think she did. There is no doubt in my mind that she lives on in me.

Experts have differing views about openness. From her interviews with dying people, Kübler-Ross came to the conclusion that most of her patients knew very well they were dying and would have welcomed being able to talk to their families about their fears and hopes. The Buddhist teacher Sogyal Rinpoche believes that heartfelt communication with others is the key to life and essential at death, and exhorts us not to be so afraid of death talk. He tells us that we do not need to be experts. We just have to be a true friend offering unconditional love, who will not react adversely if the dying person is afraid or angry. We should avoid the temptation to preach to the dying, or to give them our own spiritual formulae. What the dying person needs is to be loved and accepted as we would want to be loved and accepted if the position were reversed.

Dr Sandra Jay takes a more cautious approach. 'Hope that can be interpreted as denial is an incredibly strong emotion which helps many patients cope with dying right up to the end. I am not sure we have a right to take hope away from them.'

Doctors are on the front line and are frequently damned whatever they say or don't say. They are the ones who have to give the bad news of a terminal illness. They have to deal with the patient and concerned relatives usually in short and rushed appointments. Unless the patient is in hospital, the GP is responsible for the care of the dying person and the carers involved.

In the old days, stories of consultants and doctors delivering news of terminal illness in an insensitive manner were legion. They often took it upon themselves without consultation to tell the patient, but not the family, or vice versa. Today, medical professionals have more training in communication skills and these conversations should be better handled. But they are still very tricky. What will be experienced as honesty by one person may well be viewed as brutal directness by another. If doctors stick to the facts of the patient's condition, they risk sounding too clinical and brutal. If they are not open about the patient's terminal condition they may deny the patient and family the opportunity to discuss the options for future treatment or, in the case of the very old, for refusing further treatment.

In his book *Hippocratic Oaths*, Professor Raymond Tallis handles the dilemma as follows:

> My own rule is this: no patients should be lied to; and no patients should be force-fed information they would rather not have. Finding a humane and honest middle course that is right for an individual patient is not easy.

A sensitive doctor will try to stick to the facts when talking about symptoms and options and then wait to see how the patient responds. One person might respond by asking, 'Are you saying that I'm dying? How long have I got?' Another might show no curiosity and ask no further questions. The doctor can then respond to the cues that have been given. If a doctor knows a patient well and there is trust between them, communication will be more instinctive.

It is really important to respect the beliefs and views of patients and their families. Denial is understandable and normal and we should not tell a dying person what they do not wish to hear. We can show love and gratitude through care and attention. Deidre told me that, odd though it might sound, she and her children would not have missed the death of her husband for the world.

> It was a very natural death. Our aim was to make him as comfortable as possible. Someone was with him, holding his hand, night and day. Today there is such an emphasis on men being with partners when they have babies. I think it important that we are together at the end of life. We were there holding his hand and talking to him when he died.

Denial, however, comes at a cost, as Simone de Beauvoir recounted in her book about her mother's death:

> At the time the truth was crushing her and when she needed to escape from it by talking, we were condemning her to silence; we forced her to say nothing about her anxieties and to suppress her doubts: as had so often happened in her life, she felt both guilty and misunderstood.

Denial prevents the dying person from overtly preparing for death, and it prevents those who are close from sharing in the preparation. Provided the dying person is not suffering from dementia or delirium, tasks can be addressed which could make a crucial difference to the dying process. The grief of the bereaved can be compounded if the dead person has left affairs in a mess. These tasks might be practical or spiritual. There may be important information to impart to a partner, or children; I heard of someone who was told by her dying mother that the father she thought was dead was actually alive. There might be debts to be acknowledged or paid off. Small possessions may be labelled for special people to be distributed after death. We saw the gleeful delight with which Alistair Sampson organized his own funeral service. By choosing our own hymns and readings we can ensure that we will be very present in hearts and minds at our own funerals.

There are emotional tasks to fulfil too. There may be amends to make, or misunderstandings to clear up. If death is not being denied, important decisions can be taken about how to use the remaining time. One person might just want the company of a beloved spouse of 50 years. Another might want the whole family, including grandchildren, to be around. I know of a Scot who wanted to be taken back to the Scottish Highlands to die. He died in a room from which he could see a familiar view from his childhood.

The dying person can benefit from professional or expert support as well. In hospital the task of the medical staff is made much easier if death talk is on the agenda. The patient (if mentally alert) and the members of the family can ask questions of the doctor and discuss treatment options. In the dying phase, patients should not have to submit to further painful treatment if they and their families think this inappropriate. Some patients might want to know what will happen to their bodies as they die. A doctor should be able to give them an honest answer. Or it might be the relatives who want to ask questions and get honest answers in return.

For those with strong religious beliefs, spiritual support at the end of life can be of great solace. For Buddhists who believe in the doctrine of rebirth, mindfulness as the spirit leaves the body is important. Death is eased by the presence of a monk or sister, reciting from the *Tibetan Book of the Dead*. A priest at the bedside of a Catholic will administer the last rites known as the Sacrament of the Sick. The priest will anoint the patient with oil or holy water, give absolution for all sins committed and say the beautiful prayers for the dying. An Anglican can also receive Holy Communion and gain forgiveness for sins. Christians will receive the reassurance that they are leaving this world for eternal life in the Kingdom of Heaven. Father Mark explained his role when ministering to the dying in these words:

> For a priest it is an intense privilege to be called upon to accompany a person on this journey. The family calls in a priest to be part of their community and to give them the words and gestures at this crucial time. I see my role as twofold – first to the dying person and second to the family. In both cases it is about making the transition, which is never going to be easy, as comfortable as possible. It is about the holding of their hand in every sense to enable them to face this momentous event with some tranquillity and peace.

A belief in reincarnation helps Hindus and Sikhs to welcome death, which is eased by chanting and prayers at their death beds. Muslims want to die with their faces towards Mecca, hearing the words, 'There is no God but God, and Muhammad is his prophet.' Sometimes someone who has been in denial does want to say something just before the end. Those in attendance can be watchful for such a moment.

If the presence of a priest, pastor or rabbi is of crucial significance to the dying person, it should be arranged if possible. In the last phase it is surely unethical and cruel to impose our own views on the dying person. I heard of someone who read the New Testament out loud to a relative who was an avowed atheist. I also heard of a relative refusing to call a priest for the last rites for his devout mother because his own faith had lapsed.

Talking is not the only way we can communicate about death. Throughout the ages and across cultures, enormous creative energy has been expended on it by artists, craft workers, musicians and writers. Think of the lavishly decorated tombs in the Valley of the Kings in Egypt. Since the time of Christ artists have struggled to do justice to the subject of the crucifixion. In writing we have the sublime poetry of John Donne, who challenged the finality of death in his famous verse:

> Death be not proud, though some have called thee
> Mighty and dreadful, for thou art not so,
> For those whom thou think'st thou doest overthrow,
> Die not, poor death, nor yet canst thou kill me.

Even in twentieth-century Britain, when death became sanitized, it has been the inspiration of some extraordinary work. Benjamin Britten's *War Requiem*, which was first performed in the restored Coventry Cathedral, is a timeless memorial to the dead of two world wars. Britten composed the music around the searing poems of Wilfred Owen, who was killed a week before the Armistice in 1918.

Sam Taylor-Wood, who is one of our outstanding contemporary artists, works with photography and film. During her struggle with recurring cancer, when her own mortality was very much in mind, she produced a video entitled *A Little Death*. In this silent projection one sees the inexorable collapse, disintegration and putrefaction of a dead hare until all that is left is the fluffy white tail. The short film with its unadorned realism has the power to shock viewers.

The famous artist Maggi Hambling is fascinated by death. The theme occurs over and over again in her work. She sketched first her mother and ten years later her father when they were laid out in their coffins. A dream she had about death resulted in a series of ink sketches entitled *Mud Dream*. She had dreamt that she was lying either on earth or in water when yellowish liquid mud engulfed her. Surprisingly, the dream left her feeling positive rather than fearful of dying. A visit to Mexico, where death is celebrated in festive street parties, influenced her series of metal coffin sculptures. The controversial sculpture entitled *A Conversation with Oscar Wilde*, which was erected opposite Charing Cross Station, shows an animated and laughing figure rising out of a sarcophagus.

Film and television can be influential in challenging the taboo around death. The Spanish film *The Sea Inside* is a brave and fair attempt to tackle the subject of euthanasia. The American cult television series *Six Feet Under* is about the dysfunctional Fisher family who run a private undertaking business in Los Angeles. The family living-room and funeral parlour are separated by a single door and the lives of the living and the dead are inextricably mixed up. The episodes are at times funny, grotesque and sad but have the effect of normalizing death and its aftermath and bringing it straight into our sitting-rooms.

# 5

# Dying at home

Most of us would wish to spend as long as possible living independent lives in our own homes. If we had the choice we would also prefer to die there. Yet at the present time fewer than a quarter of total deaths in the UK occur at home. There are several reasons for this. The possibility of a home death tends to depend upon the following factors: a determined stated preference to die there rather than in hospital; strong hands-on family support; access to specialist palliative care; and a suitable medical condition.

Dying at home is a more likely option for people who have enough money to pay for professional carers or who have dedicated family and friends prepared to do the caring – resources not available to everyone. Two social changes have made caring within the family more difficult. More women have careers today which they cannot give up without affecting the family finances, and people are more geographically mobile for their jobs and become separated from elderly relatives. It is only possible to give adequate care to someone who is dying if they live together or very close by. Accommodation may be too small to offer room to an elderly relative, an arrangement which can be highly stressful anyway. The death of a loved one at home may be a first experience which makes it an intense and demanding event for the informal family carer. The uncertainty of time can be very stressful, involving as it does practical and mundane decisions such as how much time a carer needs to take off work or when relatives who live far away should be summoned. Doctors can sometimes make what is called a 'trajectory of dying' but it will only be an estimate. All these factors make it difficult for friends and relatives to care for the dying in their own homes.

All people dying at home need professional care, but not everyone needs specialist palliative care. General palliative care in the home is delivered by GPs and community nurses, who co-operate with the family carers. Specialist palliative care services are delivered by multi-disciplinary teams that include medical consultants, nurse specialists, occupational therapists and social workers. A complex plan, involving both health and social care, needs to be organized to obtain these specialist services. The trouble with these care plans is that they can be inadequate, under-resourced and prone to breakdown.

Lastly, some illnesses are easier to cope with at home than others. Patients with cancer are more likely to die at home because there is usually a defined dying stage which makes it easier for a palliative care package to be put in place. The treatment of cancer has been the most generously resourced palliative care service, largely due to charitable donations to hospices. Hospices are no longer just places where people go to die. Most of them now offer day care, respite care and advice and help in the home. In fact, nearly half of all people admitted to a hospice return home again, the average length of stay being 13 days. Macmillan nursing was set up specifically for the treatment of those with cancer. With other illnesses, such as lung, heart and renal diseases, it is much harder to anticipate the time of death and so patients frequently die in hospital. These conditions are also more complicated to manage at home.

In order to receive NHS funding and an appropriate care package to enable them to die at home, patients must fit eligibility criteria set down by their Primary Care Trust. Each area of the UK has its own guidelines and criteria for what is available through a Community Care Assessment. A care plan is likely to need constant adjustments to match the needs of the dying person. For instance, someone in the last year of life might need a weekly visit from a nurse organized by the GP, Meals on Wheels and a home help organized by Social Services, and wheelchair and bathing aids organized by an occupational therapist. Someone in the last week of life is likely to require daily visits from a community nurse, the services of a night nurse, and a special bed, mattress and other equipment. In theory, services at home are meant to be based on an assessment of patient needs. In practice, they are based on the resources available locally, which are frequently patchy and stretched. Jim considers that his mother, who died in her own home in Worthing at the age of 100, was fortunate in her local authority.

Although she lived on her own, her determination to stay in her own home kept her alive. This was recognized by her social worker who wrote this in her assessment. She got a wonderful care package which met all her needs. This was a mix of social and nursing care. Nurses popped in and out every day to check on her bedsores. She had home helps to give her meals and cups of tea and to do her housework and shopping. Visitors from voluntary organizations dropped in to make sure she was all right. She wasn't rich and the financial contribution she was asked to make was very reasonable. In any event she did not have to sell her house to pay for the care she received at the end of her life. My advice to the very old is to move to Worthing!

Lesley Barrow, a community nurse I interviewed, is very confident about the quality of care that is delivered to her patients who die at home in the area of Hampshire in which she works. She does the hands-on nursing while a care assistant helps with washing, turning and other personal needs of patients. Lesley works co-operatively with the local GP, who oversees the patient's pain-control medication. Her job has been revolutionized by the use of a battery-operated syringe driver which delivers subcutaneous analgesics, sedation and other medications. Lesley is also fully aware of how much support is needed by the relatives who are caring for the dying person.

I feel privileged to be able to do this work. For me it's not just a job. It's something I love doing. I try to treat my patients in the same way I would treat my own parents. I learn something new from my dying patients every day. I have learnt from experience that it is a mistake to know what is best for them. We all want to do things in our own way. Some people are quite open about the fact they are dying. Others don't use the word at all. I try to explore and find out what words the patient and the partner or carer are using and follow their lead. It is a huge mental and physical strain on the relatives involved in the day-to-day care. They have no idea how long it's going to go on for. 'How long will it be?' is a frequent question. And of course we can't tell them, though sometimes I can talk about the speed of the deterioration.

The nights can be very hard. We do have a night-sitting service but it is not always available. Even when I am not there, the carers know they can call me at any time.

Some patients want to know what is going to happen before they die. Again I can't predict but I say they will stop wanting to eat or drink, which is natural. We don't force them to eat or set up intravenous feeding. I tell them that they will sleep a lot and that their breathing patterns will change. Even the harsh noisy breathing caused by accretions in the lungs which people call the death rattle and which can so distress the relatives does not hurt the patient.

On the whole I find that most people die peacefully. My patients often die in the early hours of the morning. If the relatives have not been present they can be very upset but I remind them of all the times they were there. We put a lot on the relatives who care. I admire them very much. Despite the strain they are glad they have done it.

I can truthfully say that for me death is a good experience. We can get very close to our patients and feel sad when they die.

Macmillan Cancer Support is another resource that can be called upon for those with terminal cancer who are dying at home. Macmillan nurses do not provide hands-on nursing or domestic care in the home. Their main function is to give advice and support to cancer patients from the time they are diagnosed. They are also specialists in controlling pain and symptoms. They often liaise between patients, relatives and the hospital or doctor. They offer emotional support to the family carers as well as the patient. Macmillan services are free, but a GP, nurse or hospital doctor needs to make the referral. Simon felt that he and his helper Sarah could not have kept his wife at home without the assistance of the Macmillan nurse who was assigned to them when Pam was dying from cancer.

I have to say that she was an angel. My wife was watching out of the window when she came up the drive. We were expecting a matronly figure to appear. Instead there was this young girl, beautifully turned out and dressed in a mini-skirt. We immediately got the sense that she knew her business. She organized the district nurse and phoned the doctor. The district nurse taught Sarah how to dress Pam's bleeding skin sores, how to give bed baths and how to administer the medication which came first in patches, then orally and lastly via a battery-operated syringe. The Macmillan nurse came every week. She made the decisions about the pain-control medication, which she communicated to the doctor who prescribed it. She always had time to talk to us, as well as Pam.

Towards the end, after a really bad weekend, she asked Pam how she was coping. Pam, who was a direct sort of person, asked her outright, 'How long have I got?'

> The Macmillan nurse said, 'Two or three days. This is the time, if you want to see anyone, to do it now.'
>
> Pam said, 'You mean, to say sorry?' She did need to, and she did.
>
> The last three days were the worst and I think we only coped because of the help and the confidence which we got from the Macmillan nurse. She told us what to do and what to expect at every stage. And the curious thing is that she did all this without lifting a finger.

Marie Curie Cancer Care can also be part of an end-of-life care package. Marie Curie have specialist nurses as part of their teams, but unlike Macmillan they specialize in the care and support of people in the terminal stages of their illness. They have extended their support to those with HIV and Motor Neurone Disease as well as cancer. Marie Curie nurses provide hands-on nursing during the day and night. The service is free for the patient, but because half the nursing costs are paid for by the Marie Curie charity and half by the community nursing budget, the number of hours may be limited.

The NHS is making an effort to extend the reach of palliative care beyond cancer patients to include those with other illnesses, for example Motor Neurone Disease and chronic obstructive pulmonary disease. To achieve this, and to enable more people to die in their own homes if they wish, there will need to be improvements on several fronts.

Patients and their families often do not know what professional services are on offer and how best to access them. The way forward is to improve the information about available services and increase the funding for them. There should be a named individual to co-ordinate the various professionals involved in what is often a complex and rapidly changing package of care. A great deal depends on the goodwill and dedication of the family carers, who often feel ignored and neglected by the professionals involved. They need to be involved in all aspects of treatment, information and communication wherever possible.

Private care is a good option but is so expensive that it is open to only a few. Deidre managed to pay for five years of private care for her husband Malcolm, by dint of working herself and a generous contribution from her children.

Malcolm was working hard and playing tennis until the age of 85 when he started to be unwell. He had been in hospital three times with various crises to do with his heart and detested the experience. He hated losing control, which is what happens when you go into hospital. When he became seriously ill and seemed unlikely to recover we decided to keep him at home rather than put him through such distress again. He certainly felt happier in his own environment and was less aware of the serious change in his condition.

First we started with daily carers, which I got through a private agency. I could have got some help from Social Services, but I knew the carers would change too frequently and I wanted more continuity of care for Malcolm's sake and my own reassurance while I was out at work. Carers need to have breaks, so after a while I had to have two to cover for each other. In the last two years we graduated to a live-in carer. This was usually a trained nurse from New Zealand or Australia who would cook Malcolm's meals, do his personal washing and some shopping, and see to the medication. The only complaint my husband had about the carers was that they were terrible cooks. He watched endless programmes about cooking on television and dreamt of meals by Nigella Lawson. So I tried to make special efforts at the weekend.

I do realize how fortunate we were to have this level of care. It did cost a huge amount of money.

As private care can be afforded by only a small minority and end-of-life/palliative care on the NHS is still in a stage of development, it must be said that dying in our own homes does not yet amount to a realistic option for everyone who wants it. Neither is dying at home an ideal option for everyone. If the main carer is an old and infirm partner, it will be too much. Others find that the intermittent healthcare cover provided does not make them feel as secure as they would in a hospital, where there are doctors and nurses present all the time. Some do not want their loved ones attending to their intimate personal functions, or watching their deterioration at close quarters.

Those who do opt to die in the familiar environment of their own home have the satisfaction of feeling more in control of the dying process. Partners, friends and relatives may find the experience gruelling, but they have the satisfaction of caring for their loved one in comparative privacy. They too will feel more in control of events. After all, they know better than anyone what the patient likes and dislikes. A widowed friend told me how she had been able to sleep alongside her husband every night until he died, including the night of his death. 'It was such a healing thing to do. I was able to say goodbye with no one hassling me. I would never have been allowed to do this if he had died in a hospital.' Simon and Sarah knew how much Pam had enjoyed socializing, so they tried to keep life as normal as possible right up to the end.

> Two days before Pam died we had a lunch party. Friends, with drinks in their hands, wandered in and out of her room. The Macmillan nurse had told us that hearing was the last sense to go, so we went on talking and laughing around her, just as we had when she was able to respond. Pam was fortunate, and so were we, that we had the resources to let her die at home.

# 6

## Dying in a home

A care home or nursing home is frequently the last staging post for an elderly person who is living alone, or whose family carers can no longer provide the necessary level of support and supervision. Before this becomes a necessity there is a great deal that can be done to enable old people to live independently. In her book *The Good Non Retirement Guide*, Rosemary Brown gives details of all the resources available in the community to enable the elderly to live in their homes for as long as possible. These range from physical adaptations to the house, alarm systems, home helps and voluntary services like Meals on Wheels. Sheltered accommodation, available for sale or rent through private developers, housing associations or local authorities, can be a suitable compromise between independent living and a residential home. But only a few of these offer the extra care needed for those who can no longer look after themselves in their own rooms without assistance. A point comes when the next option may well need to be a residential care home.

Residential care homes, sometimes known as rest homes, are run by local authorities, by businesses like BUPA and by voluntary organizations. Admission to local authority homes can only be arranged through Social Services. The accommodation usually consists of a bedroom plus communal dining-rooms, lounges and gardens. All meals are provided, rooms are cleaned and carers are at hand to give whatever help is needed. Most homes are fully furnished, though it is usually possible to take small items of furniture. Except in some of the more expensive private homes, bathrooms are normally shared.

Although a few care homes have nursing facilities, residents may well have to be moved a second time to a nursing home when they require more intensive care. It is nursing homes that provide medical supervision and fully qualified nurses round the clock. Not surprisingly, therefore, they are more expensive than care homes. They vary hugely in price and quality and the most expensive can cost more than £1,000 a week.

The word 'home' is meant to be reassuring. Even though a care or nursing home caters for a number of residents under the care of professionals, the theory is that it should feel more home-like than institutional. It should combine the advantages of proper and secure care with the advantages of a homely atmosphere. Unfortunately, the reality does not always match the theory. All care homes should be registered by Social Services and inspected once a year, but even with these safeguards there are too many stories of neglect, if not abuse, in care homes for the elderly.

A report published in February 2006 by the Commission for Social Care Inspection found that almost half of England's nursing and care homes were failing to meet national standards on medication, staff training and record-keeping. The report found significant geographical variations in performance and indicated that council-run homes were worse than those in the voluntary and private sectors. We all have a horror of being incarcerated in a home where we could be badly cared for and over-sedated by workers who are poorly paid and not properly trained to care for the dying. Too often homes close down, forcing residents to move, often some distance away. Recently I read a tragic account of an old couple being separated after 60 years of marriage. Moving is difficult at the best of times, but for the very old it is confusing and distressing and can hasten death. Brenda's experience of a residential home was an unhappy one.

When it became clear that my parents were finding it difficult to live at home, it was decided that they should move in with my brother and his family because they had a house that was big enough. The arrangement was a disaster and I associate the onset of my mother's Alzheimer's from this time. They then moved into sheltered accommodation, which worked quite well. But they decided off their own bat to move from there into a residential home. Maybe the care of my demented mother was all getting to be too much for my father. But the home was like an institution and they simply hated it. The carers saw to the laundry and cleaning but they were really under-staffed, and looking back I believe that my mother starved to death. The carers would bring food to their room but did not help my mother to eat it. With Alzheimer's, swallowing can become a problem. My poor mother became a skeleton. The manager also disliked my father. I know he was difficult but she thought he was posh and took it out on him. I was frightened of complaining too much because I didn't want to make it worse for them. Both my parents died in the home when we were not there. I will always blame myself.

My basic advice to everyone is to do everything you can to enable your parents to stay in their own home. If that is not possible, choose a home where the manager is a loving and caring person. The home my parents died in didn't smell of pee and decay like so many of the horrible ones do, but it was cold and uncaring. You felt that immediately.

Richard too had a negative experience when his aunt, aged 83, went into a residential care home after an operation on her hip.

The home looked all right superficially, but it was the most stagnant and depressing place. To be honest, my aunt was a bit of a snob and didn't want to join the other old 'biddies', as she called them, for meals. But no effort was made to cajole her downstairs. There was no physiotherapy or massage for her leg. No one bothered to see that she took exercise. She just sat slumped in her room. To add insult to injury she was called by her first name, which she detested. It was frightening how quickly she went downhill. We took her out of there and she lived for another year in her own flat with the help of live-in carers. I know she would have died much sooner if we had left her in that dismal place.

At the other end of the scale there are exemplary homes, one of which I visited so that I could seek advice from the manager, Siobhan Shine. Otterbourne Grange in Hampshire is a private, moderately expensive residential care home for 25 residents. It is a large, rather shabby converted house set in extensive grounds. Despite the fact that the staff members are dressed in blue uniforms the atmosphere is very informal and homely. The sitting-room, which has a view of the lovely garden, is full of comfortable chairs and flowers. Residents include two dogs, a cat and a fish. The staff work hard to keep the residents stimulated and there is a lively air about the place. Visitors come and go throughout the day. These include relatives, doctors, physiotherapists, hairdressers and chiropodists. The local rector comes once a month to pray with residents and staff. The home is not at all plush and some of the residents even have to share rooms, but there is never an empty bed. The home gets daily enquiries from people who have been recommended by their doctors or by word of mouth. Siobhan has worked in the home for over twenty years and loves her job.

Unusually, this home doubles as a care and nursing home. Siobhan herself is a trained nurse and has staff members with Level 2 National Vocational Qualifications. She has a close relationship with the local doctors and district nurses so that between them they are able to look after their residents until they die.

Before Siobhan takes anyone into the home, she visits the potential resident and the relatives at home for a thorough assessment. She likes to know as much as possible about the way they live and their expectations. This visit gives the family a chance to question and get to know her too. Siobhan believes it is vital for her and the relatives to be singing from the same hymn sheet, so she is honest with them about both the advantages and the disadvantages of residence in a home. She makes sure that she knows about the family's beliefs and wishes around death so that there are no misunderstandings when that time comes.

> I do not believe there is ever a time when someone wants to give up their home. It's always a second choice to come here. People are frightened of the unfamiliarity and possible rules and regulations. They don't want to lose their independence even if realistically they've lost it already. We encourage them to bring items of their own furniture and mementos, especially photos. We also ask the families to write us a history of their relatives. It helps us so much to know what sort of lives they have led. We ask the families not to visit for a week at the beginning to allow them to settle in. And in my experience, once the decision has been made, they settle in very well. In fact, the residents who settle best are the ones who were most independent in their lives. Once in the home their horizons tend to shrink and they become less involved with the outside and more involved in the lives of the care workers and other residents. They share in all our weddings, birthdays and family sagas. Sometimes the families get upset if they take residents out and they ask to come 'home', meaning back here. We carers can get very attached to residents and miss them very much when they die.

Siobhan is matter-of-fact about death. 'Death is like birth. It is something we have to go through.' She is proud of the fact that, once in her home, residents do not have to move again, even when they become incontinent, senile or immobile. When her residents are dying, she and her colleagues aim to keep them free of pain and as comfortable as possible. They turn them every two hours, feed them with a syringe and keep their mouths moist. They explain to the relatives what they are doing and try to answer all their anxious questions honestly.

> Relatives want to know how long it will take. Are they in pain? Can they hear what we are saying? Are they aware? Are they frightened? I tell them what I know from experience, which is that most old people die peacefully and painlessly. It seems to me that they fall unconscious before they realize they are dying. They might be aware of death a while before, but not just before.

Siobhan also gave very sound advice on how to go about choosing a suitable home.

> Do not contemplate a home that is not state registered. You can get hold of the results of the last inspection. When choosing a home, try to get feedback from people who have had recent experience of it. In the first interview ask questions about staffing levels, the frequency of staff turnover and the history of the management. Beware if there have been too many changes. Inquire if there is any possibility of the home changing hands or closing down. Find out what supervision and training is given to the staff, whose job is mentally and physically demanding but who are often poorly trained and badly paid. After the initial interview it is wise to visit the home unannounced and ask to be shown around a second time. Some homes will accept the old person for a short-term visit to see if it is the right place. Ask under what circumstances the resident would need to be moved on. Homes do not always say that residents have to leave if, for instance, they become incontinent. Find out what occupational therapy is on offer, for example music, art and physiotherapy. Residents have a much better quality of life if there is a lot going on. Ask if residents are kept to their rooms or encouraged to join in communal activities. Expensive is not always best. Posh rooms with en-suite bathrooms where residents spend most of the time on their own are no substitute for social and mental stimulation. The cost of residential care can be high, so find out if there are any extra costs involved.

If a relative dies in a poorly managed nursing home, relatives can feel upset, angry and guilty, especially if they were not there at the end. But if someone dies in a good home where he or she has been happy and well cared for, the relatives will be able to accept the death, even if they missed it. A care or nursing home can be a very positive end-of-life experience for resident and family. Relatives can be relieved that the old person is in a safe place with plenty of company and supervision from a loving and experienced staff. Having lost their independence and moved into a home, some old people are more psychologically prepared for death. Others get a new lease of life from regular balanced meals and from the social stimulation and company. In order to avoid a bad home and a bad experience, relatives must carry out thorough research (if they have options) when looking for a suitable home.

Anyone who has concerns about a home can contact Action on Elder Abuse, which was founded to help prevent physical, psychological and financial exploitation and other types of abuse of elderly people. It also provides guidance and training for professionals engaged in the care of vulnerable older people. It has a free confidential helpline, offering advice and support to individuals who feel that they are victims of abuse as well as to other members of the public who have grounds for concern.

# 7

# Dying in a hospice or hospital

The reputation and influence of hospice care is huge in relation to the actual number of hospice places. In 2005 in the UK there were 221 adult in-patient units, including designated palliative care wards in general hospitals. Cancer patients will comprise the majority of patients treated in these units. The number of combined beds came to just over 3,000.

When I visited a Marie Curie hospice I was immediately struck by the atmosphere of peace and quiet. This particular hospice has 32 beds, a dining-room, several sitting-rooms, an art therapy room, a library, a computer room and a gym. In addition to palliative care offered to the dying, the hospice does rehabilitation work in a day therapy unit where patients are given help to manage their conditions before they become terminal. Complementary therapies like aromatherapy, massage, healing, hypnotherapy and relaxation are also on offer.

At the time of my visit, some patients were resting quietly in bed; others were sitting in family rooms chatting with visitors or playing with young children. Relatives and friends are welcomed day and night and can sleep on pull-out beds in a family room. Members of staff, who were not wearing uniforms, mingled inconspicuously with patients, who were also normally dressed. There was very little sign of medical equipment and even the unmistakable hospital smell was absent. It felt like a communal home rather than a hospital. I began to understand why, even though only a tiny percentage of people die in hospices, polls show that the public perceive hospice care in a very positive light.

As so much emphasis in the hospice philosophy is given to psychological and emotional support, I had a long talk with one of the trained counsellors about what sort of issues concern the dying. This is what she told me.

Patients talk to us about many concerns. They can be very distressed by the effect of illness on their bodies. They can gain weight on steroids, or lose their hair and their looks. They also have to come to terms with a loss of status. Illness has meant giving up their job and their role in the home. There are a lot of things they feel they no longer have control of. Young mothers worry about what will happen to the children they are leaving behind and how everyone will cope. Older people maybe have more concerns about the meaning of life. Some who have been religious lose their faith at this stage. Those who are not religious still question the meaning of life.

My belief is that people die the way they have lived their lives. Some are very accepting. Indeed, some old people who have been ill or in a residential home for a long time are ready to die. They are so tired of life they would hasten it if they could. Others are not so accepting. If they have been angry in life, they might be angry at the end. It is especially hard for people who have been very well and active and get a terminal diagnosis out of the blue and are given only a short time to live. They can be full of turmoil and anger, and a lot of preparation work needs to be done in a short time.

We discuss everything with the patients. They know that we do not do resuscitation or intravenous feeding. This is often difficult for relatives. In some cultures, food has great symbolism and it is hard for them to stop feeding their loved one while the body shuts down.

I feel very much for families whose loved one has a brain tumour or a disease which changes the personality. They have to deal with the death of someone who is no longer the person they knew, and this might come on top of months and months of caring. Most patients die peacefully but, to be honest, there are a few whose nerve or bone pain we cannot control, which is awful for everyone.

I am sure that the subconscious works strongly in dying people. I think that at some level they are in control of the timing of their own deaths. A person so often dies when a relative has left the room just for a short time. I comfort them by saying the loved one wanted this because of the kind of person they were or so as not to give pain. I have known patients who have waited for days, against all the odds, for a son or daughter to arrive from abroad before allowing themselves to die.

We offer bereavement counselling for six months to any family member who wants it.

Another advantage of dying in a hospice is the access patients have to complementary therapies, the provision of which is an integral part of the hospice philosophy. The symptoms of dying patients may well include fatigue, physical tension, restlessness, breathlessness, pressure or suppurating sores, constipation and pain. Therapies such as gentle massage or aromatherapy, reflexology, cranial osteopathy, acupuncture, meditation, art and music can be tremendously relaxing and helpful for pain. These therapies are greatly appreciated by users, who experience them as treats.

It is easy to overlook the fact that dying patients can be miserable about their declining appearance. A hairdo or beauty treatment can be uplifting. It was important to Dame Cecily Saunders that the quality of life should be maintained right to the end. She called it 'living to die'.

To care for the very old and dying requires special qualities, if not a vocation. It helps, but is not essential, to have a general medical training and some experience of life. Good professional carers need empathy, warmth and a deep fund of patience. Most importantly, they need to have genuine respect for the individuals they accompany on this difficult journey. By and large, the people who choose to work in hospices have these qualities.

What a contrast between the hospice and the large NHS hospital I visited next. Here it was all hustle and bustle, noise and medical activity. The uniformed doctors and nurses were highly visible and they seemed to spend a lot of time checking machinery or drips attached to the patients.

Nearly a quarter of hospital beds are taken up by those in the last year of life. The majority of these end up dying in hospital, despite their wishes to the contrary. The irony is that they are dying in the wrong place. Our large NHS hospitals are better designed to maintain vital functions and get people better than to deliver palliative care. Elderly patients seem to end up in acute hospitals almost by mistake. They are likely to have been in and out of hospital for various treatments for the last year or so. On one of these occasions they may end up dying there. They get admitted to hospital because their package of social and health care at home has broken down, or because they become so ill that they need round-the-clock attention. Hospitals aim to keep such patients on the wards for as short a time as possible. At a time when the NHS is facing heavy budget cuts, hospital managers do their best to avoid having 'bed-blockers' on the wards, with the result that old and sick patients are often prematurely sent home or back to a nursing home. The Director of the National Care Forum has complained of the strain this can put on nursing homes. 'Nursing homes are not hospices, but increasingly they are being turned into places where residents die all the time.'

Large hospitals can be dehumanizing institutions. They can become like factories where illnesses, rather than the human beings who have the illnesses, are taken care of. Research and patient satisfaction surveys have highlighted a number of indignities suffered by elderly dying patients in hospital. They cite poor communication between patients, their relatives and the medical teams. There is no privacy in the wards, and doctors are too rushed to have the sort of on-going conversations that would help patients to know more about treatment options, including stopping active treatment altogether. Poorly managed discharge is a common complaint. Elderly patients may be given medical treatment and then sent home, without appropriate support or equipment, to carers who cannot cope. They are then sent back to hospital and the cycle starts again. Pain relief is not always managed as well as it should be. In hospital medications are handed out at scheduled times, and medication to kill pain might not get continuously topped up as it would in a hospice. Elderly patients are frequently moved around, which is disorientating and confusing. When someone dies, the bed may be made up and given to someone else without explanation to the patients on the same ward. They may not get sufficient help with washing, going to the toilet or eating. Old and frail people find it difficult to pick up and guide food, especially soup, into their mouths. Hospital meals tend to get dumped on their bed tables and then swept away uneaten. Because there are no sleeping facilities for relatives in hospital, they are not always present when their loved one dies. This may also be because the ward staff miss the signs of impending death and fail to call them.

In smaller hospitals, however, the experience can be very different and much more benign. Chris was full of praise for the hospital in Hull where his elderly mother died.

Although my mother was in a ward, she had a lot of space which was arranged in such a way that it felt quite private. The staff had consistent routines and so we got to know them very well. They were never too busy to discuss my mother's condition, which they monitored closely. I was amazed at how young the nurses and doctors were, but this did not prevent them being both competent and compassionate. I believe that my mother was made as secure and as comfortable as possible. I was not there at the end but I was assured that someone was with her when she died.

Where medical teams are over-stretched and focused on curing patients, it is hardly surprising that hospital is not an optimal setting for someone who is dying. The problems, however, have been recognized, and some excellent initiatives are being carried forward. An increasing number of NHS Trusts are funding palliative care teams whose task it is to support ward doctors and nurses in caring for the dying. Some hospitals contain designated palliative care wards; others have some palliative care beds on the general wards. The patient is still the responsibility of the specialist consultant, but the palliative care team can give advice about pain control and the management of nausea, constipation or diarrhoea which can cause such misery to dying patients.

The consultant palliative care nurse I interviewed said that communication with the patient and family was a high priority for all members of his team, which includes a chaplain. They find out the patient's wishes, needs and anxieties and try to address these. He reminded me that there are people who prefer to die in hospital because they have had out-patient treatment in hospital for a long time and have grown to know and trust the staff.

Another way in which the model of hospice care is being transferred to acute hospital settings is through the introduction of the Liverpool Care Pathway (LCP). This protocol, which was pioneered in the Royal Liverpool Hospital, has become a widely used model of good practice for dying patients. When a medical team switches to the Liverpool Care Pathway, in effect the current treatment programme is abandoned in favour of care and comfort protocols to ease the patient's dying phase.

Judy saw the benefits of the LCP during the time she spent visiting a very old friend from her church.

Mary was in hospital for a month. She had been in and out before that but this time I knew she would never come out. For most of this time she had been having invasive treatment. She was always being taken downstairs for examinations. Nurses came to take her temperature and stick drips in her without telling her what they were doing. Her meals were dumped on her table out of her reach. I made a fuss about this. They didn't have time to listen to what she said. Her voice had gone and you had to bend right over to hear. The doctors kept cheerfully telling her, 'We'll soon have you back on your feet.'

Another friend and I did get to speak to the doctors about what was happening. At last they put her on the Liverpool Pathway. It felt like a sigh of relief when they stopped doing things to her. She was able to let go more. She stopped eating and began to slip in and out of consciousness.

I think the important thing I was able to do for her then was not deceiving her about what was happening. I gave her a holding cross which she loved and we said prayers together. I also tried to make her as comfortable as possible. I propped her up when she slumped over and kept her parched mouth moistened. On one of my last visits I said, 'Mary, can you open your eyes?' and she opened them and I said, 'I think the eyes are the window of the soul,' and she agreed.

What can be done to help the elderly who die in hospital? It would make a great difference if every hospital had its own palliative care team. We cannot blame doctors and nurses for finding it easier to talk about symptoms than emotional issues, but some training in how to communicate with dying patients would not come amiss. On a personal level, relatives and friends can do what Judy did for her friend Mary and attend to some of the practical tasks themselves. They can make the bed and cubicle as homely as possible. They can help with feeding, interpret for the loved one who might have hearing or speaking problems, and summon assistance if needed. If the old person is being sent home, it is important to communicate with the discharge team to make sure that the home situation is tenable.

Hospitals are very daunting places which inhibit even the most confident from speaking up. Sometimes it is necessary to be assertive on behalf of a relative. For example, some ethnic or religious patients might have special needs in hospital that are not being observed. Muslims need to wash before prayers, have dietary requirements and are extremely modest. Sikhs will not be parted from the five symbols of their faith, which must be about their persons or near their beds. Relatives should not be reticent about acting as advocates or complainants on behalf of their dying relatives.

Relatives can help doctors act in the patient's best interests if he or she becomes unconscious or unable to communicate. Alternatively, the doctor might need to help the relatives accept the situation. It is at this point that a Living Will or Advance Directive can be a useful reference point in any decision to discontinue medical intervention. The key to achieving a good death in a hospital setting is all-round communication, for which time, space and opportunity must be found.

# 8

# The role of informal carers

The role of partners, relatives and friends in the end-of-life care of the elderly should not be underestimated. There are over six million informal carers in the UK, who constitute an army of dedicated unpaid workers. If government had to pay the equivalent amount of money to cover the cost of this care the national budget would be seriously affected. The magnitude of the task some family carers undertake cannot be overestimated either. Caring, as well as being cared for, can be difficult and demanding, giving rise to ambivalent feelings on both sides. An old person who has been active and in control can find it almost unbearable to be dependent on others. Janet told me how much her father had suffered from the indignities of old age.

> My father had been able to look after himself until a year before he died. He had a brilliant memory and was a voracious reader. The first serious blow to his morale was when he started to go blind. Television wasn't a solace because he hated it anyway. Then he became immobile and got gloomier and gloomier and couldn't talk about anything except how he wanted to die. There was nothing I or the grandchildren could do to cheer him up. The worst thing was when he became incontinent. He found this so distressing and humiliating that he would weep. I can't say that I found it easy to deal with incontinence pads either.

Family carers under the most strain are those who are looking after sufferers from dementia. As we grow ever older and as medical science begins to get a successful grip on one set of diseases like cancer and AIDS, other diseases gain ground. The main cause of dementia is massive cell death in nearly all parts of the brain and is a gradual, progressive and irreversible disease affecting the loss of higher mental functions. The most common form is Alzheimer's Disease. The first stages include forgetfulness, withdrawal and bewilderment. From there it progresses to short-term memory loss, disorientation, loss of inhibition, confusion and loss of ability to perform common everyday tasks. It may go on for years, but if no other illnesses supervene it eventually causes death.

In his book *Elegy for Iris*, which was made into a film, John Bayley has written a compassionate account of his wife Iris Murdoch's struggle with dementia. When Iris was still lucid she described the onset of Alzheimer's Disease as 'sailing into darkness'. It was a terrible struggle too for John Bayley, who cared for her as long and as best as he could. He gives sardonic descriptions of the mortification involved in the loss of mental capacity. Trying to get Iris to change her clothes for bed or for a swim in the river was an ordeal that nearly overwhelmed him. He found her constant anxiety and endless repetitions maddening. He suffered from watching the disintegration of his wife's famous intellect and imagination.

He got wry amusement from the thought that both of them could get moments of respite by watching the UK children's programme *Teletubbies* on television. He found her irrational habit of over-watering the plants and picking up scraps, worms and twigs from the road hard to bear, and was ashamed of his occasional outbursts of rage. And while he did not complain, it is obvious that he felt overwhelmed and exhausted most of the time.

This book gives a taste of the physical and mental burden undertaken by family carers who may well be elderly themselves. The worst aspect of all is the loss of a familiar and beloved person. Dementia changes personality, compounding the stress for carers. It can be extremely depressing if a well-mannered old person loses inhibition and becomes rude or aggressive.

A major difficulty for carers of old and sick relatives is that the responsibility tends to fall on them at the wrong time in their lives. The majority of family carers are women who might well be holding down jobs, looking after children and managing two households. Or they might have completed their parenting roles only to find themselves tied up all over again by duties and responsibilities that are frequently frustrating, boring and exhausting just as they were starting to enjoy their new freedom. If the caring falls on the shoulders of an elderly partner, the task is likely to be overwhelming.

The uncertainty of time is an important factor too. If someone is diagnosed with terminal cancer, death will occur in a manageable time frame which enables relatives to rally round and cope. With dementia and other progressive diseases, carers may find themselves burdened for years without knowing when the end will come. Some families do manage to share the responsibilities of caring, but the main burden often falls to one individual, which can lead to feelings of resentment. In fact, carers often experience a range of negative emotions which make them feel uncomfortable and guilty. They feel bad about being angry and frustrated with a loved one who can't help being dependent. Yet it is only human to have such feelings, and acknowledging them can be helpful.

Janet admitted to finding incontinence a trial. This is a normal reaction. To witness the physical decline of a parent whose habits become slovenly and whose hygiene is lacking is extremely painful. Richard found the mental decline and change in character of the beloved aunt he had removed from the gloomy care home very hard to bear.

> She had always been a joy to visit because she had been so lively and interested in everything. In the last year before she died, she grew progressively more depressed, uninterested and morose. She just turned in on herself. Also the manner in which she became rude and aggressive towards her professional carers was quite embarrassing. It was most uncharacteristic of her, though she had never suffered fools. Funnily enough, she was never like that with me. Visiting became a duty rather than a pleasure and I felt relieved to get away.

Another honest person told me how agonizing she had found visits to her dying mother in hospital.

> It took me two hours to drive to the hospital and two hours back. I did this without complaint, but once I got there I could barely sit still for half an hour and spent some of this time chatting with other patients in the ward. My mother didn't seem to care whether I was there or not. When she did speak it was a jumble of events and people I had never heard of. I suppose her mind was wandering back to her childhood but it hurt me nevertheless. When she was failing and I was called by a nurse to hurry to the hospital, I found myself praying for it all to be over quickly. I feel ashamed of myself but I am just not good at this sort of thing.

In a family memoir called *Hidden Lives*, Margaret Forster was distressed by the fact that her mother died a disappointed and discontented woman. Her constant refrain was, 'I've had enough. I want done with it. It hasn't amounted to much, my life.'

Not everyone is good at dealing with the old and dying. It can be just too difficult, demanding or painful. Acknowledging the feelings can help, but it does not always take away the guilt. Family members can feel racked with guilt if they put their elderly relatives into a home, especially if, as often happens, the move appears to hasten death. They can justify the decision on reasonable practical grounds but are still left with the feeling that they are being selfish and disloyal.

Why, then, are so many people in this country caring for their old relatives despite the stresses and strains? Money is sometimes a consideration. Looking after someone at home is cheaper than paying professional carers or nursing home fees. But this is not the main motivation. Families care for their old folk out of a sense of duty and obligation. They feel it is the right thing to do. They also do it because they feel love and gratitude. Larry's motivation is a common one.

> It never occurred to us to put my mum in a home. She had been a good mother to me and my brothers and we were not going to throw her on the scrapheap when she couldn't look after herself. As we had the largest house it fell upon us. I don't think it would have worked if my wife hadn't been so supportive. She looked after Mum as if she was her own.

The reward for people like Larry is that their grief after death is likely to be uncomplicated. He and his family felt that they had paid their dues and done the best they could. Guilt was not an emotion with which they had to contend.

Learning to care can benefit all members of a family. Grandchildren often build up wonderful relationships with grandparents, and I have been told countless stories of the compassionate and practical assistance they have contributed. In a society which has a casual attitude to the elderly, perhaps as adults they will retain a respect for the old and vulnerable.

Dr Sandra Jay believes that, towards the end, family members can help their dying loved ones a great deal if they themselves can 'let go of them emotionally'. Resistance and distress can be easily transmitted to a dying person. When Dylan Thomas wrote his famous poem 'Do Not Go Gentle into that Good Night' he was exhorting his old father not to die.

> Do not go gentle into that good night,
>   Old age should burn and rave at close of day;
>       Rage, rage against the dying of the light.

Elisabeth Kübler-Ross takes a contrary view:

> Those who have the strength and the love to sit with a dying patient in *the silence that goes beyond words* will know that this moment is neither frightening nor painful, but a peaceful cessation of the functioning of the body.

Carers need some care and attention themselves. Far too much is put upon them and expected of them. In the future, in order to cope with the increasing number of old people, more public resources will be needed to help them. As it is, there are more resources out there than is generally realized. Even a bit of extra assistance can be a lifeline. *The Good Non Retirement Guide* is a mine of information about what is available. Age Concern and Help the Aged will advise carers whether they are eligible for an attendance allowance and how to get supplementary assistance from their Primary Care Trusts and Social Services. The organization Carers UK provides useful information on carers' rights and access to support services. Voluntary organizations, for example Contact the Elderly, find volunteers to visit and help out. Day centres and clubs for the elderly, organized holidays, short-term placements and Good Neighbour schemes could provide carers with the short bursts of respite needed to keep them going.

The Michael Sobell Centre in north London, run by Jewish Care, is a model of its kind. The elderly are transported to and from the day centre. They are offered tea, coffee and lunch throughout the day. In addition there are varied opportunities for learning, including computer skills, music, arts and crafts. Day centres are no longer places where the old sit in silence staring into space. They are kept stimulated, however disabled they may be. They can also talk to sympathetic people about their worries and anxieties. While the old person is being well cared for in a day centre, the family carer can have a much needed day off.

Carers, too, might need to talk with someone who understands their problems. The Relatives and Residents Association offers a support service to families and friends of older people concerned about long-term care. There are local groups around the country where relatives can meet and discuss any practical or emotional worries they may have about opting for residential care. Those who feel they could benefit from bereavement counselling after the death of a loved one can contact Cruse Bereavement Care.

# 9

# After death

One of the characteristics of a death in the UK is the amount of bureaucracy it entails. As soon as someone dies, a number of practical requirements need to be addressed. A free booklet entitled *What To Do After a Death* can be obtained from the local Social Security office. The *Which?* book *What To Do When Someone Dies* is another excellent and practical guide. If the dead person has left papers and affairs in good order in an accessible file, the practical and administrative tasks ahead will be much easier for the relatives. For some bereaved people these tasks are a welcome distraction and afford a breathing space for the loss to sink in. For others, the bureaucracy feels like a burdensome intrusion into their grief.

## Verifying the death

If an old person's death is expected and occurs quietly at home, the first thing to do is to inform the GP. There is no need to call the emergency services. If someone dies peacefully in the night it is not necessary to inform the doctor until the morning, which gives the bereaved time to grieve privately and stay close to the body. The doctor will say whether it is necessary to verify the cause of death. If the doctor has seen the patient within the last 14 days and knows that death was due to natural causes, he or she can sign the medical certificate of the cause of death without even visiting the house. If the doctor does not intend coming, be sure and ask for his or her permission for a funeral director to remove the body, which may not be done otherwise. The doctor might decide to view the body later at the undertaker's mortuary. If a cremation is intended, the doctor must view the body either at home or at the undertaker's and must arrange for a second doctor from a different practice to view the body and sign the second part of the certificate of the cause of death.

If the patient died in hospital and no family member was present, the next of kin will be informed as soon as possible. If the death is natural, the certificate of cause of death will be routinely signed by the duty doctor. If death is unexpected or occurred during or after an operation, the coroner must be informed and an investigation undertaken. If death occurs at night time the body will be moved to the hospital mortuary and an appointment made with the relatives to deal with the formalities the next day. The deceased's possessions will have to be removed from the hospital and collected from the property office. The relatives must arrange for the body to be collected from the hospital mortuary by a funeral director.

## The relatives' role in organ donation

If the patient has died on a life-support machine in an intensive care unit, an organ co-ordinator may well approach the relatives, whether or not that person had signed up as an organ donor. If the patient is a registered organ donor and has died on a hospital ward, the nurse in charge will inform the organ co-ordinator. The co-ordinator will talk to the relatives and leave written information with them before the specialist team takes over. The body can be viewed afterwards in an open coffin if required, and the funeral arrangements are not affected. Should a donor die in a nursing home, corneas, tissue and bone can be removed, provided the body is sent to a hospital mortuary. If a whole body has been donated, the medical school with whom the arrangements have been made will have the body collected (with the proviso that it is suitable for research purposes) by their con-tracted funeral director. It is the responsibility of the medical school to arrange and pay for the burial or cremation (according to the wishes of the family) when the appropriate time comes.

## The 'first' or 'last offices'

Most of us will then follow convention and arrange for an undertaker to come and remove the body so that the 'the first offices' will take place in the funeral home. At the first meeting the funeral director will have a full discussion about all ensuing procedures with the relatives who wish to be present. Most of the practical decisions need to be made at this time. Experienced funeral directors are usually very skilled at dealing with disorientated and emotional clients. Some of them may even have acquired counselling skills qualifications. Funeral director Neil Sherry is the sixth generation in his family business. He is extremely proud of his profession. 'A funeral is very personal. It is a one-off event which has to be right.' An important decision that has to be made is the choice of a coffin from a range of designs, woods and prices in a catalogue.

Then there is the question of viewing. Neil Sherry explained that fewer than half his clients choose to view the deceased today. Many of these are from ethnic cultures where until recently the laying out of the dead was done in the home. Bodies can be viewed in a hospital chapel, or later in the chapel of rest in a funeral home. The decision to view the body is very personal and no one should be forced to do so. The experience of seeing the dead body of a loved one can be emotionally disturbing. On the other hand, the majority of people to whom I spoke found the experience deeply significant. As one woman put it to me,

> I was not with my mother when she died. I was shocked when I saw her laid out in her coffin in the funeral home, but it made me realize for the first time that she had really gone. There was no doubt about that when I saw her lying there. She was there but not there, if you see what I mean. The viewing was a form of closure and in a way made the actual burial much easier.

Jim, whose mother died in Worthing, was able to view his mother's body in the hospital chapel where she had been laid out. 'Doing this was very important to me. I had not been present when she died and this visit helped me to accept the finality of her death and say goodbye.'

If a body is to be laid out for viewing, a funeral director will recommend that it be embalmed. Neil Sherry's great grandfather Henry Sherry was responsible for disseminating modern embalming techniques in this country after extensive travels in the USA. So impressed was he with the procedure that he organized a series of lectures demonstrating the benefits. Later he formed the British Undertakers Association, which became the National Association of Funeral Directors.

Embalming is not only done for hygienic reasons of preservation but because the dye makes the corpse look pinker, younger and firmer, though some people prefer to remember the deceased as he or she was in life, with all the hallmarks of natural ageing which gave the person so much individuality. Neil Sherry believes that it is a solace for the bereaved to take away a peaceful image of their loved ones. As embalming is a skill which has to be learnt, it is a costly item on the final bill. Funeral directors do not always make it clear that embalming is optional, let alone unnecessary nowadays when bodies can be kept in a hygienic state in refrigerated cabinets. Embalming may be advisable if the body is going to be viewed, but it is mandatory if a body is being repatriated. However, it should be borne in mind that a body will not be accepted for a green burial if it has been embalmed.

A subject that can cause upset because it is such a personal matter concerns clothes for the deceased. Relatives will be asked to bring a garment from home unless they wish to choose a gown from the undertaker's catalogue. The opinion of funeral director Barry Albin-Dyer, as quoted in a *Guardian* article, is interesting. He admits to feeling sad when he is asked to put new shoes on the deceased. 'Because they are going nowhere are they? Whereas if you put on shoes that that person wore, they have seen life, they have seen and trod this world.' Relatives should also be aware that pacemakers must be removed if cremation is intended.

Families who have opted for a DIY funeral will be undertaking the 'first offices' themselves. They can obtain advice from *The Natural Death Handbook* which gives detailed instructions on how to wash the body and anoint it with oils. This must be done in the first four to six hours before rigor mortis sets in. It is important to keep the room and body as cool as possible. Those who have had no previous experience may be disconcerted when parts of the body begin to discolour with purple blackish patches. This is due to blood settling in the lower parts of the body. Hindus, Sikhs, Muslims and Orthodox Jews regard the laying out of the deceased as a religious duty. Tending the body involves closing the eyes, tying up the chin, straightening the arms and legs, washing and dressing the body in prescribed shrouds or garments. If the death occurs in a hospital, a nurse will respectfully lay out the body with the help of family members if they wish to participate. In hospital this is referred to as 'the last offices', as opposed to 'the first offices' in a funeral home.

## How to register the death

A provisional date only should be made for the funeral because it cannot take place until the death is registered at the Registry of Births and Deaths, usually housed in the local town hall. To avoid wasting time, it is sensible to make an appointment first. Only when the registrar issues the formal death certificate and the disposal certificate can the funeral take place.

The person who registers the death is known as the informant and is usually a relative or someone who was present at the death. The funeral director cannot accept this responsibility. In addition to the doctor's certificate(s), the informant will have to give the following particulars: the date and place of death; the name and surname of the deceased, including the maiden name for a woman; date and place of birth; occupation; name and occupation of spouse or civil partner; date of birth of surviving spouse or civil partner; usual address; and whether the deceased received a pension from state or public funds. It is wise to get several copies of the death certificate at the same time as these will be needed when dealing with banks and insurance companies. Once a death has been registered, the registrar issues a green certificate (the disposal certificate) authorizing either burial or cremation. This certificate should be given to the funeral director, who will take it to the church, cemetery or crematorium officials; they, in their turn, must inform the registrar when disposal has taken place.

## Post-mortems

Delays and complications in these routine procedures will take place if the coroner has to be involved. The coroner is responsible for discovering the cause of a sudden, accidental or suspicious death, and may require a post-mortem, which at the present time can be done without the consent of relatives. During a post-mortem the body is opened up and the organs examined to ascertain the cause of death. The body is carefully sewn up and can be viewed afterwards by relatives. If death has occurred in hospital, however, the consent of relatives to a post-mortem must be obtained.

A post-mortem can be helpful to the bereaved if the evidence shows that nothing could have been done to prevent the death, but the reverse could happen if it becomes clear that an avoidable mistake has occurred. The requirement for a post-mortem can itself cause deep distress to relatives, especially those from religious and ethnic groups who find this a violation of the human body and therefore abhorrent.

The registrar cannot issue the death certificate or the green certificate until the coroner's report has been received, which may cause a delay.

## Obtaining probate

It is important to let a number of people know about the death immediately. The Department for Work and Pensions must be informed in order to deal with any pensions. The deceased's bank or building society must be notified. Some families want to put a notice of the death in a national or local newspaper; this is expensive but can be a useful way to make details of the death and the funeral arrangements more widely known.

If the deceased has made a will, the executors will have been appointed and soon after death they should start the process of getting legal authority to carry out the will, known as obtaining probate. They may organize all this themselves or go to a solicitor. Depending on circumstances, there may be a delay of up to two months for the grant of probate, during which heavy expenses can be incurred. These will include funeral costs, probate court fees and possibly inheritance tax which has to be paid before probate is granted, although banks and building societies will generally do their best to release cash as a temporary measure to cover these expenses. A surviving spouse may have to get the executor to arrange an overdraft from the deceased's bank for temporary living expenses.

The executors must then produce an account, with professional valuations if necessary, of what the deceased owned at the time of death. These assets include money in the bank, stocks and shares, land and properties, as well as personal possessions like books and pictures. The threshold for inheritance tax currently stands at £285,000. If no tax is owed then probate can be obtained quite quickly, but if affairs are complicated it may take months.

Once the final reckoning is reached, it is possible to work out what inheritance tax (if any) is owed to HM Revenue and Customs. This tax is initially only paid on the proportion of the estate representing personal property. Tax on land will not be collected until some time later. Forms and guidelines for working out the tax can be obtained from the Probate Registry, and Revenue and Customs will also work out what tax is owed. Once the initial payment of the tax due has been arranged, an application for probate can be made in a probate registry. The papers, which must include the will and the tax receipt, can be sent by post, but the executor (or executors if there are two) must attend an interview when probate is granted to receive authority to start carrying out the terms of the will, including the payment of legacies.

## Funerals

Meanwhile, arrangements for the funeral will be in train. The Co-operative Group and Dignity are the biggest single providers of funerals in the UK, collectively accounting for a quarter of all funerals. Independent funeral directors make up the rest. Among the independents are many firms that have been in the hands of the same family for generations. The best way to choose a funeral director is ask around for a personal recommendation from a friend or relative who has had a good experience. If the preference is to use a small firm rather than one which is part of a large chain, it is better to choose one that is a member of the Society of Allied and Independent Funeral Directors (SAIF).

Those who contract an undertaker to organize the funeral should be aware that they can pick and choose from a range of services. A funeral director can be paid to do everything from locating a pastor to arranging an obituary, choosing the flowers, organizing the service and seeing to the catering for the post-funeral gathering. Alternatively, the funeral director can arrange the hearse and the burial or cremation, while the family attends to the obituary notices, flowers, catering and order of service. Those who have been regular attenders in a church will want to have their own minister leading the service.

However sympathetic a funeral director might be, it must be borne in mind that organizing a funeral is a business transaction, and a competitive one at that. Sales mean profits and undertakers can be skilled salesmen. They can make suggestions and exert subtle pressure at a time when the bereaved are disorientated and grief-stricken. For the bereaved who want to give their loved one a spectacular send-off, expense may not be an issue. They are prepared to pay extra for hearses drawn by motorcycles or plumed black horses, a fleet of black limousines, mountains of flowers, baskets of doves (to be released at the critical moment) and musical bands, all rather reminiscent of traditional funerals in New Orleans.

Others may feel they are spending more than they would like or is necessary on an expensive coffin and flowers out of embarrassment at being thought mean and shoddy. As Timothy explained,

> When my mother died seven years ago, the option of coffins was put to me in such a way that I would have felt like Scrooge if I had chosen a simple pine coffin with plastic handles over the silk-lined oak coffin with brass handles.

Beth recollected how embarrassed she had been when she overheard relatives commenting negatively about the use of a cardboard coffin for her brother's cremation. 'I wish we had thought of making a public announcement that he had expressly asked to be buried this way. It made perfect sense because he was a keen organic gardener.'

Jim had a good experience with the undertaker he contacted in Worthing.

> The local funeral director was recommended by my mother's Unitarian pastor. He proved both respectful and businesslike. He was dressed in black and met me off the train with a funeral pack to hand. He told me how to register the death, how to arrange for the body to leave the hospital, and how to buy a plot in the graveyard. We were shown a catalogue of coffins starting with the cheapest. He recommended a florist and a gastro pub where we could have the post-funeral reception. My experience with this particular undertaker was a good one. There was no pressure to spend more money than was necessary and the final bill was very reasonable.

No one should feel too harassed or embarrassed to shop around for estimates and ask for a breakdown of costs. Reputable undertakers are members either of the National Association of Funeral Directors (NAFD) or of the Society of Allied and Independent Funeral Directors (SAIF). It is bodies like these who try and prepare the funeral industry for problems in the future, such as threatened restrictions on emissions from crematoria or the banning of embalming fluids. They operate a Code of Practice and are obliged to produce a detailed list of costs. The estimate for the funeral account will be in two parts: first, the fees that the funeral director will charge for collecting the body, arranging the first offices, supplying the hearse, cars and bearers, and arranging and conducting the funeral, whether it is in a church or a crematorium; and second, the fees that go to third parties, such as doctors' fees for cremation certificates, crematorium or burial fees, and fees for the church, minister, organist, gravediggers, obituaries and flowers.

All these additional costs can add up to a significant sum. In recent years many of the small family funeral directors have been taken over by large American companies, and the rise in funeral costs in the last five years has been so steep that concern has been expressed in the Houses of Parliament on several occasions.

Funeral directors who are association members are obliged to provide a basic funeral for those in financial difficulties. They can also give advice as to whether there is a possibility of a grant from the Social Fund, though this is governed by strict criteria.

Those who want a Christian funeral should first contact a minister before booking a time and date for the service with either a church or a crematorium. This can take some days, which allows time for the music and order of service to be arranged. For the funerals he conducts, Father Mark encourages the full participation of the bereaved.

I ask the family to sit round the table with me and to talk about the loved one who has died so that they can remember what sort of person he or she was and so that I can understand what the loved one meant to them. I want them to do a real and deep review of the events of that person's life. I always ask for something that brings a smile to their faces. My job in the funeral itself is to bring people from the blackness of grief to the dawn of hope. During the service I first acknowledge the pain of loss and then move on to the message of hope which is the lifeboat the bereaved can cling to in the sea of grief.

Christians have a vast fund of sublime hymns, prayers and Bible readings for the funeral service. I know from experience what a difference a carefully arranged service can make to the bereaved. While writing this book I dug out a pile of printed programmes of the funeral services I have attended over the years. I find that among these the most popular hymn has been Psalm 23, 'The Lord is My Shepherd'. And the most popular prayer, which is often sung, is:

God be in my head, and in my understanding;
God be in mine eyes, and in my looking;
God be in my mouth, and in my speaking;
God be in my heart, and in my thinking;
God be at mine end, and at my departing.

In the case of a DIY funeral, the family will be seeing to most of the details themselves, though it is possible to use a funeral director for some services like transport. The body can only be kept at home for a few days without refrigeration, so it will be necessary to make arrangements to leave it in the hospital mortuary, store it with an undertaker or send it to the council's public mortuary.

The most basic and cheap biodegradable coffins are made of cardboard or chipboard. The elaborate ones woven from willow or bamboo are more expensive. A much more expensive but delightful option is to commission an artist to paint the coffin with an individual design or theme. Alternatively, it is a good idea to buy a plain coffin and paint it at home. This can be a therapeutic activity for children. Some people like to construct their own coffins before they die. Others have relatives who have sufficient carpentry skills to make a home-made coffin for them after they have died.

The vehicle to transport the body must be large enough to carry the coffin. A rehearsal may be in order, because handling a coffin is not as easy as it looks.

The funeral cannot take place, whether in a church, crematorium or natural burial site, unless all the required certificates are in order.

Non-believers who want a dignified but individualistic funeral can seek advice and assistance from the British Humanist Association, who will send an officiant round to your house to create an appropriate ceremony. These may be conducted at crematoria, cemeteries and woodland burial grounds.

Muslim communities normally appoint one person to represent them in making funeral arrangements with an approved local funeral director. Many council cemeteries now have designated areas for Muslim burials. Muslims may not be cremated and should be buried in a white sheet within 24 hours in an unmarked grave which is raised from the ground. Regulations in this country insist that the body is transported to the cemetery in a coffin.

Hindus are always cremated. In India and Pakistan these cremations would take place on open pyres. The burning of the dead body signifies the releasing of the spirit and the flames represent the presence of the god Brahma. In the UK such open pyres are forbidden, though the Anglo-Asian Friendship Society continues to campaign for a change in the law to allow traditional cremations to take place. The Asian Funeral Service arranges Hindu funerals and organizes repatriation of the body for those who can afford a funeral by the Ganges. Sikhs too are cremated. After death, Sikh men are dressed in a white cotton shroud, older women in white and young women in red. The deceased is taken home and the coffin opened so that family and friends can pay their respects. The body will then be taken to the Gurdwara (temple) for a service before going to the crematorium. A Sikh is cremated with five precious symbols from which he can never be separated. The oldest son, who traditionally would have lit the pyre, presses the crematorium button instead. The elders of the Gurdwara will advise on which funeral directors are appropriate.

Jewish funerals are governed by a set of rituals and traditions, particularly applying to the seven immediate members of the deceased's family. The family should first notify the deceased's rabbi, who will guide them in the necessary procedures. The burial should take place quickly and be as simple as possible.

The funeral symbolizes a significant change in the family system. With the loss of a parent the middle generation steps up to take the lead. Taking responsibility for the funeral arrangements makes this transition clear and concrete. The funeral can also act as a catalyst for the strengthening of family bonds that have weakened over the years. Sometimes half-siblings or distant relatives meet for the first time at funerals and are able to make up for lost time. For grandchildren, this might be the first significant loss they have experienced. They will be learning a great deal about death through witnessing the sadness of family members and by participating in the funeral. An appropriate funeral both honours the dead and enables the bereaved to express their grief. As Neil Sherry said, it is well worth the effort to get it right.

# 10

## Memorials

Before, during and after the funeral, the relatives and friends of the person who has died are grieving. Grief is the physical, emotional and psychological way in which we express our pain and sorrow when we lose someone or something to which we are deeply attached. It can be seen as nature's way of helping us to deal with separation and loss. We should expect to suffer when something precious is removed from us. Grief affects different people in different ways through a process that changes over time.

Grief in relation to loss can be experienced on a rising continuum of intensity. At the minimal end are the normal losses, like leaving home, with which we deal as we pass through transitions in the life cycle. Through these we gain the strength, resources and confidence to help us withstand the more challenging losses that come our way, for example divorce, redundancy or illness. At the intense end of the continuum comes bereavement, which is the death of someone close to us. But even with bereavement some deaths are easier to absorb than others. For example, a sudden or accidental death, a suicide or the death of a child is likely to be more traumatic than a natural death.

The death of an elderly relative at the end of a long life should give rise to normal, if painful, grief. The death is natural in that it is the end of the life cycle and will have been more or less expected. In some cases, the death of an old person after years of illness, senility or immobility may come as a relief. The old person will be sorely missed, but the younger generations must get on with their lives.

The most traumatic grief is likely to be experienced by a partner in a long-standing relationship. If two people have been closely attached for 50 years or more, the death of one can have a huge impact. Indeed, it comes as no surprise if the remaining partner dies shortly afterwards.

We experience grief as a jumble of emotions which might include shock, denial, anger, pining, anxiety and sorrow. Grief can be physical, too, affecting sleep, appetite, concentration and memory. There will be good days and bad. After some months the emotional intensity will lessen and the number of good days will increase.

Painful though grieving may be, the majority of us do get through the process. We reinvest in life again, while maintaining positive and happy memories of our loved ones. But there are some individuals who get stuck in what the experts call complicated or abnormal grief. They may suffer from physical complaints, drink too much or become reliant on tranquillizers. They may become severely depressed and contemplate suicide.

Why do some people have trouble recovering from grief? They may have had insecure attachments in their childhood that make losses hard to bear. They may become overwhelmed by a series of big losses. They may have been over-reliant on the person who died. Sometimes the bereaved are prevented from moving on by a sense of guilt because they had a difficult relationship with the deceased or did not do enough for them at the end of their lives. Anyone suffering from intractable grief should consult a doctor or psychiatrist.

There are plenty of positive ways we can find to help the grief process along. We can talk to supportive friends and family about our feelings for the person we have lost. We can look after ourselves physically by eating well and taking exercise, which will have a good effect on our emotional state. We can join a support group or see a bereavement counsellor if we want another perspective. And we can seek spiritual sustenance from religious leaders. In addition to the important ritual of having a funeral, we can create memorial occasions that will allow us to express our loss in a structured and concrete way in the future. What we do for the dead we are really doing for ourselves.

## Memorial occasions

We are familiar with memorial services for the great and the good in St Martin's-in-the-Fields and Westminster Abbey, but we don't have to be rich or famous to have one ourselves. A memorial service or gathering can be organized some months after the funeral. While the funeral service focuses more on loss and grief, a memorial service is a celebration of the life of the person who died. The atmosphere is more light-hearted and there is room for levity and humour. The timing between the two is crucial, as Miranda explained to me.

> I was so overwhelmed with grief and shock when my husband died I sort of crawled through the funeral. There was no way I could have organized or appreciated a more public ceremony at this time. Six months down the line, though, I was in a different place. My sons helped me to arrange a memorial service in our local church. Friends and colleagues had plenty of notice and the church was packed. It was wonderful to know that so many people cared about John. An old friend from university and a cousin gave tributes which contained stories about him that I hadn't heard before. To my utter astonishment it was an occasion which I enjoyed.

We can organize memorial occasions in all manner of venues. I heard of one held in a pub at which someone had been a regular: the deceased was remembered with affection while pints were downed. A friend of mine whose husband had been a non-believer held a gathering for friends and relatives, the purpose of which was to share memories about his life. His oldest friend told some amusing stories of his school days. Another described him as a work colleague. A Palestinian spoke warmly of the charity work he had done in the Middle East. By the time everyone had finished speaking, a rich portrait of a talented and generous character had been developed. One of his sons made a recording of the meeting.

## Epitaphs

For families who have chosen a burial for their loved ones, the choice of a headstone containing the epitaph or inscription is another staging post in the bereavement process. The more thoughtfully it is done, the more meaningful it will be. Another gathering at the graveside can be organized when the headstone is set in place. For Jews, the erection of the headstone in a ritual known as 'stone-setting' takes place after eleven months, and has special meaning because it marks the end of the period of official mourning.

In past centuries, especially the nineteenth, extravagant funeral monuments with elaborate epitaphs were fashionable. In the old section of Kensal Green Cemetery in London there are some extraordinary mausoleums and constructions that are well worth visiting. The granite or marble gravestones are decorated with weeping angels, draped urns and even elephants! Kensal Green was the first of the great commercial cemeteries to be opened in London. It is entered by a large Doric arch and was designed around three gravelled roads wide enough for carriages. The central avenue leads to the Anglican chapel, beneath which are extensive catacombs still in use today.

Before he died in 1826, Thomas Jefferson designed an obelisk and inscription to mark his own grave at Monticello. Of all his achievements, he wanted to be remembered as

> Author of the Declaration of American Independence,
> Of the statute of Virginia for Religious Freedom,
> And father of the University of Virginia.

Oscar Wilde, who died disgraced and in exile in France in 1900, has a particularly sad epitaph:

> And alien tears will fill for him
> Pity's long-broken urn,
> For his mourners will be outcast men,
> And outcasts always mourn.
> (Père Lachaise cemetery, Paris)

Monuments on this scale would be considered in bad taste today. In any case, parish churches and municipal cemeteries now have strict rules about the measurements, materials and even the wording of headstones. The most common format for modern epitaphs consists of the heading 'In Loving Memory of', followed by names and dates and sometimes descriptions such as 'Beloved Father' or 'Dearest Mother'.

The funeral director should be able to warn clients what restrictions are in place. The firm may also provide their own masonry service. If not, they will certainly recommend local stonemasons. Names can also be obtained from the National Association of Memorial Masons. In addition to the cost of the headstone, a fee will be charged for putting it in place, on top of the charge for the exclusive right of burial and the interment fee.

Some people are prepared to pay more to have unique epitaphs created by skilled designers and engravers. Harriet Frazer's association, Memorials by Artists, was inspired by the experience of her own family being greatly helped by the creation of a unique and beautiful headstone for her step-daughter, who committed suicide.

In view of possible rules and regulations no one should commission a memorial without checking carefully first. As the cost of memorials varies hugely, depending on the type of stone, size and lettering, it is important to ask for a written estimate with a breakdown of costs, including delivery and erection charges.

It is wise to wait several months before erecting a headstone to allow for the grave to settle. The delay also gives the family time to think about an appropriate inscription if the deceased had not already planned one.

Epitaphs in crematoria are more restricted. Shortly after the cremation has taken place, a brochure will be sent to the next of kin explaining the available options for which there will be an extra charge. The most popular is the Book of Remembrance. This is a large illuminated book which is permanently on display in the crematorium. Inscriptions of the name, date of death and a short epitaph are inscribed by hand in the book, the pages of which are turned on a daily basis. Some crematoria have a columbarium, which is a colonnade of niches for ashes. Others have space in the chapels or passages for small metal memorial plaques. I spotted a plaque in Croydon Crematorium which I liked for its simplicity: 'Danny Piggott 1927–1997. Croydon's greatest dustman for 31 years.' Rose trees with metal plaques at the base may be planted in a designated area in the grounds.

Inscriptions permitted by crematoria are so standardized that people often prefer to take the ashes away with them and dispose of them in a more individualistic way. I have seen a beautiful metal sculpture of a heron in somebody's garden. It marks the place where the ashes of a beloved son are buried. Some football and cricket grounds have designated areas for the ashes of faithful spectators. Keeping the ashes in an urn on the mantelshelf at home might give comfort to some but is liable to accident or disaster. There is a hilarious scene in the film *Meet the Parents* when the hapless young man (Ben Stiller) knocks over the urn containing the grandmother's ashes by misdirecting a champagne cork. This did not prove a good way to impress the potential in-laws.

The dead can also be memorialized in other ways. For a fee, many public parks can help organize the planting of a tree with a plaque, or a named bench. Recently I sat on Hampstead Heath upon a wooden bench inscribed with the name and dates of a man who had loved walking there. As I sat admiring the view and watching children playing with kites and dogs, I thought what a delightful memorial his family had chosen for him.

Obituaries can be placed in national or local newspapers and on the internet. They are brief summaries of the life and achievements of the deceased. The best are packed with interesting anecdotes which convey the essential character of the subject. In February 2006, Radio 4 started to broadcast obituaries in its programme *The Last Word*. Both national and local newspapers have ready-prepared obituaries that are immediately printed when someone prominent dies. Otherwise, there is nothing to stop anyone offering an obituary in the hope that it will be accepted. The *Guardian* encourages people to send in signed obituaries for its column entitled 'Other Lives'.

On-line obituaries are open to everyone and have the advantage of being more interactive. They also feel more personal and immediate than printed ones and can reach a wider audience for a longer period of time. Memorials in cyberspace really came to prominence after September 11th, 2001, when a website called Legacy.com was set up to memorialize the victims of the terrorist attack on the World Trade Center and Washington, DC. As the list of names grew, so did the personal tributes and condolences that gradually accumulated in the 'Guest Book'.

A search for memorials on the internet will bring up various sites, some of which are free. The most sophisticated offer facilities for customized design, the creation of photo albums, personal stories, contact lists for friends and family, automatic reminders of anniversaries and a chat room. The obituary can be accompanied by the deceased's favourite music.

Money is often raised by the bereaved and donated to a charity in memory of a loved one who has died. Sometimes relatives request a contribution to a specific charity rather than flowers for the funeral.

People like to organize sponsored memorial walks because it is a lively activity involving many in a common cause. I know someone who sponsors an annual performance by a youth orchestra in memory of her musical husband. Such charities as Cruse, the Samaritans and the Royal Marsden Hospital rely heavily for funds from people who have lost family members and want to give something back to the organizations that cared for them.

## Anniversaries

Anniversaries of the death provide an occasion for further rituals. In the ceremony called the Yahrzeit, Jews light a special candle on the anniversary of the death of a close relative. While the candle burns for 24 hours, the Kaddish, which is the prayer for the dead, is recited. Catholics can light candles and have masses said on the anniversary of a death. A family might visit the woodland site where the burial took place for an annual picnic. The anniversary can provide the impetus to tend the grave and lay fresh flowers. Or a family might just gather together in a private way to share a meal and memories of a loved one.

In some countries the national Day of the Dead is celebrated with a holiday. The Chinese holiday of Qing Ming Jie is held in April. This day is also known as 'tomb sweeping day' and is marked by an annual family gathering at the ancestral graves, where offerings are laid and fireworks set off. In Mexico, the Dia de Muertos is the most important celebration in the year and a popular tourist attraction. It is a joyous occasion, being a festival when the souls of the dead are invited back to participate in pleasures they had known in their lives. It is marked by heavy drinking, street dancing and colourful processions. Even young children dress as skeletons or carry skulls. The ceremonies are not only public: in private homes, too, an offering of food and drink for the dead is laid out on a table decorated with flowers and candles.

Christians traditionally celebrate the Day of the Dead on 31 October, the eve of All Saints' Day, but this date is no longer widely regarded as an occasion for prayers for the dead. Instead we associate it with Hallowe'en pranks and parties – rituals which hark back to pagan witchcraft.

The Natural Death Centre is hoping to popularize a national Day of the Dead in the UK. They hold an annual weekend in April in which events relating to death are organized. The aim is to remember the dead and to reflect on death in a positive rather than morbid atmosphere. It remains to be seen whether this idea catches on.

For those who believe in an afterlife, there is the consolation of knowing that their loved ones live on as spirits or in reincarnated form. The desire to communicate with the departed spirit can be so strong that some bereaved people turn to spiritualism, using a medium for telepathic communication with the loved one. At the turn of the twentieth century, spiritualism was very popular and quite respectable. Even Sir Arthur Conan Doyle, who created in Sherlock Holmes the most rational of detectives, became a public exponent of the benefits of spiritualism. His own son, along with thousands of other young soldiers, was killed in World War I and buried abroad without any of the rituals that help the bereaved deal with grief. In these circumstances it is hardly surprising that the bereaved turned to spiritualism. They must have needed reassurance that their loved ones were all right. Even today spiritualism seems to help some people get over a significant death. Those who do venture down this path, though, should be wary of charlatans who pretend to be psychic so that they can prey on the vulnerable.

Another way in which we remember the dead is through the memories and stories we recount about them. Some of these stories take on a mythical quality. One such story in my family concerned my grandfather, who worked as a missionary in China for many years. During a period of unrest, the only word he sent to his worried family in England was a request for a British Rail timetable. As a child I loved hearing this story and used to speculate on why he would have wanted a train timetable in China. Perhaps it made him feel less lonely. The picture that I have created of him is of a good if rather eccentric character who cared very little for material things, though I am the proud owner of a Chinese teapot that came down through the family.

I am always struck by the vivid family stories that unfold week after week on *Antiques Roadshow*. As an old clock, an agricultural implement, a furled flag, a row of service medals or a musical toy is presented to the experts, a vivid portrait of the original owner tends to emerge – a picture that has been faithfully passed down through the generations.

The more positively we live our lives, the more likely we will be to accept death, and the more benign will be the memories we leave behind. Buddhists know this when they teach that death is a mirror in which the entire meaning of life is reflected.

# Conclusion

I hope that, in writing such a practical book, I have not appeared to trivialize death. I know that for most of us it is likely to be the most frightening, challenging and difficult event we have to face in our lives. But we do not have to sit back and wait for it to happen to us. There are some ways in which we can anticipate and prepare for it.

We have seen how a general consensus for the basic requirements for a good death has been gradually building. We need to be given the option of knowing when death is coming and to understand what can be expected. We need to be able to choose where to die. We should be allowed to express our fears, anxieties and emotions in our own way. As long as we are competent, we should be able to participate in the decisions concerning our care. Even when we are old or severely ill we have a right to be heard and our wishes and opinions heeded. We want to be pain-free and cared for, but not kept artificially alive when it is clear that we are dying.

Our informal family carers should be given as much help as possible, especially as they are saving government money. The professionals concerned in end-of-life care should be compassionate, sensitive and knowledgeable people. We expect to be treated with respect and dignity as human beings even if we are mentally and physically incapacitated. We should be able to have whoever we choose at our death beds, and access to any spiritual and emotional support required.

These are in fact basic principles of good palliative care. Although the need to improve and expand the provision of palliative care has been recognized, much more progress will be needed before these requirements are converted into automatic rights for every dying person. It is not sufficient to be one of the lucky old people who live in the right postal code. On the political level, we need to encourage representative organizations like Age Concern and Carers UK to continue their stout efforts to lobby government on behalf of old people and their end-of-life needs. We need more hospice beds, palliative care teams in hospitals, and palliative care provision in the community so more people can die at home.

On a personal level there is much we can do to gain more control over our own deaths. We can try and prepare ourselves mentally and emotionally to be more accepting of the ageing process and the inevitability of death. We can make practical preparations in the shape of financial provision, wills, Advance Directives and funeral plans. The process of doing this will be of inestimable benefit to us, as well as to those we leave behind.

It is only human to want to be remembered with affection, and even gratitude. We can leave this to chance, or try to influence the way we live and the way we die.

# Useful addresses

**Action on Elder Abuse**
Astral House
1268 London Road
London SW16 4ER
Helpline: 0808 808 8141
Website: www.elderabuse.org.uk

**Age Concern England**
Astral House
1268 London Road
London SW16 4ER
Helpline: 0800 00 99 66
Website: www.ageconcern.org.uk

**Age Concern Northern Ireland**
3 Lower Crescent
Belfast BT7 1NR
Tel.: 028 9024 5729
Website: www.ageconcernni.org

**Age Concern Scotland**
Causewayside House
160 Causewayside
Edinburgh
EH9 1PR
Helpline 0800 00 99 66
Website: www.ageconcernscotland.org.uk

**(Age Concern Wales)**
**Age Concern Cymru**
Ty John Pathy
13–14 Neptune Court
Vanguard Way
Cardiff CF24 5PJ
Tel.: 029 2043 1555
Website: www.accymru.org.uk

**Alzheimer's Society**
Gordon House
10 Greencoat Place
London SW1P 1PH
Tel.: 020 7306 0606
Website: www.alzheimers.org.uk

**Asian Funeral Service**
209 Kenton Road
Harrow
Middlesex HA3 0HD
Tel.: 020 8909 3737

**Association of Natural Burial Grounds**
C/o The Natural Death Centre
12 Blackstock Mews
Blackstock Road
London N4 2BT
Tel.: 0871 288 2098
Website: www.naturaldeath.org.uk

**Britannia Shipping Company for Burial at Sea Ltd**
Unit 3, The Old Sawmills
Hawkerland Road
Collaton Raleigh
Sidmouth
Devon EX10 0HP
Tel.: 01395 568652

**British Association for Counselling and Psychotherapy**
BACP House
15 St John's Business Park
Lutterworth
Leics LE17 4HB
Tel.: 0870 443 5252
Website: www.bacp.co.uk

**British Humanist Association**
1 Gower Street
London WC1E 6HD
Tel. 020 7079 3580
Website: www.humanism.org.uk

**Buddhist Society**
58 Eccleston Square
London SW1V 1PH
Tel.: 020 7834 5858
Website: www.thebuddhistsociety.org

**Carers UK**
20–25 Glasshouse Yard
London EC1A 4JT
Tel.: 020 7490 8818
Website: www.carersuk.org

**Citizens Advice Bureau**
Addresses in local phone books or log on to www.citizensadvice.org.uk

**Contact the Elderly**
15 Henrietta Street
London WC2E 8QS
Tel. 0800 716543
Website: www.contact-the-elderly.org

**Counselling and Psychotherapy in Scotland (COSCA)**
18 Viewfield Street
Stirling FK8 1UA
Tel.: 01786 475140
Website: www.cosca.org.uk

**Cruse Bereavement Care**
Cruse House
126 Sheen Road
Richmond
Surrey TW9 1UR
Helpline: 0870 167 1677
Website: www.crusebereavementcare.org.uk

**Department for Environment, Food and Rural Affairs (DEFRA)**
Nobel House
17 Smith Square
London SW1P 3JR
Helpline: 08459 33 55 77 (9 a.m. to 5 p.m., Monday to Friday)
Website: www.defra.gov.uk

**Dignity in Dying**
13 Prince of Wales Terrace
London W8 5PG
Tel.: 020 7937 7770
Website: www.dignityindying.org.uk

**Elderly Accommodation Counsel**
3rd Floor
89 Albert Embankment
London SE1 7TP
Tel.: 020 7820 1343
Website: www.eac.org.uk

**Funeral Planning Authority (FPA)**
Knellstone House
Udimore
Rye
East Sussex TN31 6AR
Tel.: 0845 601 9619
Website: www.funeralplanningauthority.com

**Help the Aged**
207–221 Pentonville Road
London N1 9UZ
Tel.: 020 7278 1114
Website: www.helptheaged.org.uk

**Hospice Information**
Hospice House
34–44 Britannia Street
London WC1X 9JG
Tel.: 0870 903 3903
Website: www.hospiceinformation.info

**Human Tissue Authority**
Ground Floor
Finlaison House
15–17 Furnival Street
London EC4A 1AB
Tel.: 020 7211 3400
Website: www.hta.gov.uk

**Jewish Bereavement Counselling Service (JBCS)**
8–10 Forty Avenue
Wembley
Middlesex HA9 8JW
Tel.: 020 8385 1874
Website: www.jvisit.org.uk

**Law Society of England and Wales**
Law Society Hall
113 Chancery Lane
London WC2A 1PL
Tel.: 020 7242 1222
Website: www.lawsociety.org.uk

**Law Society of Northern Ireland**
Law Society House
98 Victoria Street
Belfast BT1 3JZ
Tel.: 028 9023 1614
Website: www.lawsoc-ni.org

**Law Society of Scotland**
26 Drumsheugh Gardens
Edinburgh EH3 7YR
Tel.: 0131 226 74
Website: www.lawscot.org.uk

**Macmillan Cancer Relief**
89 Albert Embankment
London SE1 7UQ
Macmillan CancerLine: 0808 808 2020 (9 a.m. to 10 p.m., Monday to Friday)
Website: www.macmillan.org.uk

**Marie Curie Cancer Care**
89 Albert Embankment
London SE1 7TP
Tel. 020 7599 7777
Website: www.mariecurie.org.uk

**Memorials by Artists Ltd**
Snape Priory
Snape
Suffolk IP17 1SA
Tel.: 01728 688934
Website: www.memorialsbyartists.co.uk

**National Association of Funeral Directors (NAFD)**
618 Warwick Road
Solihull
West Midlands B91 1AA
Tel.: 0845 230 1343
Website: www.nafd.org.uk

**National Association of Memorial Masons**
1 Castle Mews
Rugby
Warwickshire CV21 2XL
Tel.: 01788 542264
Website: www.namm.org.uk

**National Council for Palliative Care**
The Fitzpatrick Building
188–194 York Way
London N7 9AS
Tel.: 020 7697 1520
Website: www.ncpc.org.uk

**National Council for Voluntary Organisations**
Regent's Wharf
8 All Saints Street
London N1 9RL
Tel.: 020 7713 6161
Website: www.ncvo-vol.org.uk

**NHS Organ Donor Register**
UK Transplant
Communications Directorate
Fox Den Road
Stoke Gifford
Bristol BS34 8RR
Organ Donor Line: 0845 60 60 400
Tel.: 0117 975 7575 (administration)
Website: www.uktransplant.org.uk

**Natural Death Centre**
12 Blackstock Mews
Blackstock Road
London N4 2BT
Tel.: 0871 288 2098
Website: www.naturaldeath.org.uk

**Registration of Births, Deaths and Marriages**
Phone numbers in local phone directories

**Relatives and Residents Association**
24 The Ivories
6–18 Northampton Street
London N1 2HY
Helpline: 020 7359 8136 (9.30 a.m. to 4.30 p.m., Monday to Friday)
Website: www.relres.org.uk

**Royal National Institute of the Blind**
105 Judd Street
London WC1H 9NE
Helpline: 0845 766 9999
Website: www.rnib.org.uk

**Society of Allied and Independent Funeral Directors (SAIF)**
3 Bullfields
Sawbridgeworth
Herts CM21 9DB
Tel.: 0845 230 6777
Website: www.saif.org.uk

**UK Parkinson's Disease Society Tissue Bank**
Division of Neuroscience and Mental Health
Imperial College London
Faculty of Medicine
Charing Cross Campus
Fulham Palace Road
London W6 8RF
Tel.: 020 8383 4917
Website: www.parkinsonstissuebank.org.uk

***Which?***
Castlemead
Gascoyne Way
Hertford SG14 1SH
Tel.: 0845 307 4000
Website: www.which.co.uk

# Further reading

Bayley, J., *Elegy for Iris*. St Martin's Press, New York, 1999.

Brown, R., *The Good Non Retirement Guide*. Kogan Page, London, 2006.

de Beauvoir, S., *A Very Easy Death*. Penguin, Harmondsworth, 1969.

Donne, J., *The Complete English Poems*. Penguin, Harmondsworth, 1971.

Dylan, T., *The Poems of Dylan Thomas*. J. M. Dent, London, 1952.

Emerson, S. (ed), *In Loving Memory*. Little, Brown, London, 2004.

Forster, M., *Hidden Lives*. Viking, London, 1995.

Gilbert, S., *Death's Door: Modern Dying and the Ways We Grieve*. W. W. Norton & Co., New York, 2006.

Kessler, D., *The Rights of the Dying*. Vermilion, London, 1997.

Kübler-Ross, E., *On Death and Dying*. Simon and Schuster, New York, 1997.

Kübler-Ross, E., and Kessler, D., *Life Lessons*. Simon and Schuster, London, 2001.

McCullough, D., *John Adams*. Simon and Schuster, New York, 2001.

Moody, R., *Life After Life*. Bantam, New York, 1983.

Nuland, S., *How We Die*. Alfred A. Knopf, New York, 1994.

Rinpoche, S., *The Tibetan Book of Living and Dying*. Rider, London, 1998.

Simpson, R., *Before We Say Goodbye*. HarperCollins Religious, London, 2001.

Tallis, R., *Hippocratic Oaths*. Atlantic Books, London, 2004.

Tugendhat, J., *Living With Loss and Grief*. Sheldon Press, London, 2005.

Weinrich, S. and Speyer, J. (eds), *The Natural Death Handbook*. Rider, London, 2003.

Woodward, J., *Befriending Death*. SPCK, London, 2005.

# Index